Muriel Spark

Muriel Spark

Peter Kemp

BARNES & NOBLE
BOOKS
10 East 53d St., New York 10022
(a division of Harper & Row Publishers, inc.)

Published in the U.S.A. 1975 by:
Harper & Row Publishers Inc.,
Barnes & Noble Import Division

First published in Great Britain 1974

Copyright © 1975 Peter Kemp

ISBN 0 06 493619 8

Printed in Great Britain

Contents

Acknowledgments

I should like to thank Muriel Spark and Macmillan & Co. Ltd. for permission to quote from the novels; and to express a considerable debt of gratitude to David Grylls for some most valuable suggestions as to style and content made while the book was still in manuscript.

I
Economic Resources

An accomplished liar, Muriel Spark is very much concerned with truth; chronicling disruption, her books urge harmony; communicating seriousness, their tone is witty; rich in plot and generously stocked with detail, they are thrifty, frugal, economic. This is a fiction, as its author recognizes, that is based upon a principle of 'nevertheless'—something she elaborated once in an article about her birthplace, Edinburgh:

> I have started the preceding paragraph with the word 'nevertheless' and am reminded how my whole education, in and out of school, seemed even then to pivot around this word. I was aware of its frequent use. My teachers used it a great deal. All grades of society constructed sentences bridged by 'nevertheless'. It would need a scientific study to ascertain whether the word was truly employed more frequently in Edinburgh at the time than anywhere else. It is my own instinct to associate the word, as the core of a thought-pattern, with Edinburgh particularly. I can see the lips of tough elderly women in musquash coats taking tea at MacVittie's enunciating this word of final justification, I can see the exact gesture of head and chin and gleam of the eye that accompanied it. The sound was roughly 'niverthe-lace' and the emphasis was a heartfelt one. I believe myself to be fairly indoctrinated by the habit of thought which calls for this word. In fact I approve of the ceremonious accumulation of weather forecasts and barometer-readings that pronounce for a fine day, before letting rip on the statement: 'Nevertheless, it's raining'. I find that much of my literary composition is based on the nevertheless idea.[1]

Caught in a different and deceptive thought-routine—one structured around 'therefore'—critics have often failed to appreciate this, and gone on to travesty the books. These novels, it has been pointed out, |are highly artificial: therefore, the assumption goes, they must lack authenticity. Multiple instances of malice and aggression crowd the narratives: and so the author is dismissed as irresponsibly detractive. Books so entertaining, it is felt, must be proportionately trivial. A writer obviously skilled at the graphic reproduction and satiric survey of a wide variety of social surfaces can be denigrated, almost automatically, as lacking depth. And the most widespread fallacy has been that the verve and panache of these novels are indicative of frivolous intent. The response of Ivy Compton-Burnett to one of the books is, in this respect, representative: 'The Girls of Slender Means I enjoyed as a joke until it stopped being a joke.'[2] To read Muriel Spark in this way is to mistake the varnish for the picture. Her books are never simply jokes, though they invariably contain them; they are not eccentric jeux d'ésprit, ephemeral and whimsical. Comic, it has to be stressed in any approach to these novels, does not equate with trivial, any more than solemn does with valuable. It is a commonplace to describe certain works as deeply serious: the books of Mrs Spark are deeply funny, engaged, for all their wit, with very sombre themes, and everywhere controlled by strong beliefs about a novel's nature and significance.

'Fiction to me,' she has explained, 'is a kind of parable. You have got to make up your mind it's not true. Some kind of truth emerges from it, but it's not fact.'[3] Novels, as she sees it, are valuable untruth; those engaged in writing them, 'professional liars'[4]; the art they exercise, 'very like the practice of deception'[5]: and in keeping with this view, she defines her own books bluntly as 'a pack of lies'.[6] To approach them looking for naturalism, then—fidelity to the usual, steady reflection of all the probabilities—is to invite disappointment. Mrs Spark, writing always with an eye to her own axiom that if fiction 'is not stranger than truth, it ought to be,'[7] makes little attempt to camouflage her novels' artificiality. Her fictions are stylized. She is working within a convention, and the quality most clearly stamping this convention is economy—a term used often in her writing and invariably accompanied by a nod of approval. In her novels, intricately wrought and consciously artificial as they are, she is not primarily concerned with portraying character or holding the mirror up to life, though, as she continually and memorably proves, she can do both these things effectively. What she is setting out to do is to give useful pleasure by displaying a theme—generally some observation of wide relevance: 'I hope that a plot's got something universal in it,'[8] she has said—with wit and economy, anything extraneous to it being elegantly pared away.

For the most part, these books are short; always, they are neat and concentrated. The societies that attract Mrs Spark's sharp-eyed attentions are never, as in life, sprawling and heterogeneous: they are limited and specialized. 'When I become interested in a subject, say old age,' she has explained, 'then the world is peopled for me—just peopled with them. And it's a narrow little small world, but it's full of old people, full of whatever I'm studying.'[9] The way in which each novel is confined to its microcosm varies. Sometimes, the characters are restricted in place—trapped together on a desert island, members of a hostel or a school, workers in a suburb of south London, employers and employees in a secluded mansion. More frequently, they are linked by some shared quality, some attribute common to all the group—old age, obsession, celibacy. Always, though, together they comprise a closed or semi-closed society, each of the novels presenting a different and almost self-contained community. Then, like Nicholas Farringdon, her poet-martyr in *The Girls of Slender Means* (1963), Mrs Spark imposes 'upon this little society an image incomprehensible to itself.'[10] For, though she is an efficient worker on the satirical surface, acidly etching in her characters' absurdities and vices, mapping with bitter relish the forms of social savagery rampant amongst them, she is really—and here she resembles another of her protagonists, Sandy Stranger, author of that 'odd psychological treatise on the nature of moral perception'[11]—far more concerned with what she calls 'The Transfiguration of the Commonplace,'[12] the way in which these people, their traits and their manoeuvrings, can be invested with a semi-allegorical significance.

The literary ancestry for this is interesting and slightly unexpected. Asked once in interview which writers had influenced her most, Mrs Spark replied, 'Well, those I have read deeply are Proust, Newman, and Max Beerbohm'[13]—an uneasy trio, it may at first be thought, but one on which she has insisted.[14] And despite the surface incongruity of this unlikely grouping, there is a basic aptness in her naming of these writers, the work of each being strongly coloured by some different quality of prime importance to her own. Newman, for instance, played his part in leading her to Rome—'he was', she has said, 'a tremendous influence'[15]; to him she owes her interest in, and ultimate conversion to, Catholicism: and between Mrs Spark's religion and her fiction the links are very close. From Beerbohm she derives a strong concern with style, a sharp awareness of the idioms of others and a striving after what she calls 'subtle English prose with the shorter words the better and a nice witty turn to it all'.[16] She shares with him, besides a marked aptitude for parody, the mandarin detachment of her prose, a style that is invariably lucid, but also heightened, formal, conscious of itself. The claim made by her fellow-writer, Iris Murdoch—'Most modern English novels . . . are not *written*. One feels they could slip into some other medium without much loss'[17]—is very far from true of Mrs Spark. In translation or, simply, dramatized, stripped of their narrator's voice, her books must lose, and heavily.

The final major influence, that of Marcel Proust, is not immediately obvious. It is, however, fundamental. Speaking of the strong impression made upon her when she read *À la Recherche du Temps Perdu*, Mrs Spark explained: 'although he goes on in this one novel for twelve volumes I think him a most economical writer and I still have a kind of passion for Proust. I can lift down any volume and read it, and then I feel the need to create—myself.'[18] And what precisely she finds so stimulating about Proust's work is crucial, since it lies, as a point of departure, behind her own novels. In an early article, published some time before she turned to writing fiction and called 'The Religion of an Agnostic', Mrs Spark usefully singled out what was, for her, the particular significance of Proust. He was, she wrote, 'one who, in his thirty-sixth year, withdrew from a flourishing life in society in order to contemplate its inner decadence, and to whom those very symbols of decay yielded their permanent essence, restored in eternity'.[19] What we find in Proust, she feels, what is so valuable about his work, is 'the idea that the visible world is an active economy of outward signs embodying each an inward grace'[20]; this is writing, she claims, which derives power from 'an acceptance of that deep irony in which we are presented with the most unlikely people, places and things as repositories of invisible grace'.[21] Interpreting 'grace' here as something very close to what is usually referrred to as 'significance' or 'meaning', it can be said that, on this same idea, this acceptance, her own novels are built.

In them, too, unlikely people, unexpected places, contemplated and sardonically portrayed, become beautifully satisfactory symbols, yield up latent import and are shown to be endowed with essential consequence.

'I found,' Mrs Spark has said, describing her reactions on turning to the writing of full-length fiction after the poetry and criticism she had earlier attempted, 'that the novel enabled me to express the comic side of my mind and at the same time work out some serious theme.'[22] With her second book, *Robinson* (1958), standing slightly apart from the formulation, this is the way her fiction always operates: there is the satiric presentation of a carefully limited society, witty depiction of its closely scrutinized inhabitants, ironically accurate notation of the speech-inanities, social and private rituals, current in the circle under observation—Mrs Spark's ear for the damningly characteristic turn of phrase is as sharp as her eye for the give-away detail, her attention poised continually for the detection and exposure of what she calls 'those revelatory tones and gestures'[23]—and, simultaneously, the commonplace being transfigured, the 'figurative meaning piled upon the literal,'[24] this little world takes on a microcosmic quality, its tenants a significance they themselves may not understand. The surface details of the life-styles on display always seem authentic, but they have beyond this—and here the importance lies—an appropriateness to the theme of the book. 'Very true and very apt,'[25] Suzi Ramdez remarks at one point in *The Mandelbaum Gate* (1965): and the line could stand as epigraph to the whole of Mrs Spark's fiction. There is an impressive accuracy—she is a very knowledgeable writer—in the wide variety of scenes she paints—Edinburgh in the Thirties, London between VE and VJ days, Jerusalem at the time of the Eichmann trial—but, more than this, there is a relevance about them. And as her work matures, the setting, both in time and place, of each astringent narrative comes to fit more and more closely, more and more satisfyingly, its theme. The result is both true and apt, amusingly accurate and disturbingly significant. Working on a small scale, the writer is able to make large statements, for this is an art always on the lookout for: 'the image, the gratuitous image/Miserly seized.'[26] And, once seized, this image is worked until it yields all possible resonance: so a girls' hostel, depicted in meticulous satiric detail, can become a symbol of human effort to live communally and decently without aggressive competition, events during a Jerusalem summer act as metaphors for the way men are divided, against each other and within themselves.

Despite her tape-recorder ear, her penetrating and retentive eye, Mrs Spark is not attempting to give the illusion of life, for, in her terms, life itself can be illusion, dangerously obscuring basic truths by its swarming welter of diverse phenomena. She writes, she has pointed out, 'always in the hope that everything will be said and done more clearly and more appropriately than in real life'.[27] And so, in her books, there is, behind the verisimilitude, a structure and a neatness that moves her art away from naturalism into the realm of the stylized and the self-contained. Though her material is taken with some shrewdness from the life, the use she makes of it, what she selects and how she organizes this, is openly artificial. Carefully disrupting normal chronology—since 'Only a materialistic conception of Time—a strictly chronological one—could have obliterated that understanding of matter which acknowledges outward and changing forms to be invisibly and peculiarly "possessed", each after its own kind in a spiritual embodiment'[28] —making great play with time-shifts, flash-backs, glimpses forward, she attempts to bring to light fundamental patterns scribbled over by the gaudy scrawls of contingency, essential truths buried under human trivia, truths that man neglects at his own peril. Skilfully, using pattern and selection, reliant on strongly centripetal plots, Mrs Spark endows the little world she is so exactly picturing with an additional dimension, changes it from something formless and contingent into an entity possessing the meaningful and necessary design of a work of art. Having scrutinized the society she is to concentrate upon for what she would call its 'essence', she then so structures her plot, so chooses her characters and choreographs their actions, as to make this stand out vividly: the dictatorial behaviour of an Edinburgh schoolteacher in the Thirties thus becoming emblematic of Fascism; a scandal in the Roman film-world, with its subsequent circus of spurious publicity, standing as garish image of man's efforts to deceive and self-deceive. Mrs Spark herself compares her art to parable. In fact, it also comes close to allegory, to that type of writing much favoured in the Middle Ages, where the visible scene, concretely presented, is regarded as a kind of text, a fund of metaphor, which, properly interpreted, can yield important truths. In Mrs Spark's fiction, the depicted society, precisely and humorously portrayed, becomes too a potent symbol of some fundamental tenet: a tenet, usually, indicative of human limitation, for these novels are ironic as well as allegorical.

And satire, indeed, is what the books first seem to be concerned with. When Mrs Spark's characters posture, deceive, act corruptly, they do so in the shadow of the Four Last Things. Mortality hangs in these novels like a backcloth, keeping people and their lives continually in sane perspective. The unavoidable realities of time, age, death throw into relief the futility of the characters' behaviour, the brevity of the rewards they are pursuing with such misguided ingenuity. The transience of life is always stressed and its deceptive nature, filled, as it can be, with distraction and delusion, underlined. Sometimes, in the earlier works, these unwelcome facts kept nervously behind the daily scenery of existence are allowed to break disturbingly through the reassuring surface in the form of troubling supernatural incident: an uncanny tempter who wreaks havoc in a stagnant suburb, disembodied voices that remind the reluctant old of death. Later, this element tends to become more muted, yet in all the books, aware of it or not, the characters are shown—like Daphne du Toit, dancing in 'The Go-Away Bird'—as moving to 'the strains of

The fundamental things apply
As time goes by.'[29]

Yet the technique is never simply reductive. Mrs Spark's insistence upon eternity and the eternal verities may mock at much held to be of value by 'the solemn crowds with their aimless purposes, their eternal life not far away'.[30] At the same time, however, it considerably increases the significance of human choice and action. Her characters, seen ironically as erring and at times ridiculous, are also figures of important truths. They are both satirized and taken very seriously. Her treatment of them is the same as that which she attributes to Proust, saying that he 'satirizes them in the flesh by the same method that he exalts their essence, under that "aspect of eternity" which is also the aspect of art'.[31]

The equation made here is an important one for a full understanding of Mrs Spark's intentions as a novelist. Over and above the theme conveyed, the technique of these novels has for her its own significance. It is an artistic activity and it is also, as she sees it, something very close to a religious one, being an eloquent reminder of a corresponding economy inherent in the Christian attitude to life. In his memoir of the writer, Derek Stanford recalls that she once told him 'how the Catholic view of the heavens seemed to her very much more economic,'[32] and Mrs Spark herself has said that, after entering the Catholic Church, she 'began to see life as a whole rather than as a series of disconnected happenings'.[33] The bearing on her fictional technique is not hard to recognize. Searching first for the heart of the matter, for what a given situation can reveal of God's intents and purposes, the novelist is trying to discover and then more clearly to display meaningful patterns already present in life—'I believe events are providentially ordered,'[34] she has said—patterns of whose existence the easier structures of her art are intended to make us beneficially aware. The fictive organization is regarded as reflecting on a small and comparatively simple scale the vaster and more complex dispositions of divinity. According to Catholic belief, life is very far from being meaningless flux; everything is necessary, nothing contingent; people are, as it were, characters in a novel they themselves construct; man's choices are loaded with significance—'the next few eternal minutes are important'[35]; 'our conversation is in Heaven'[36]; he writes himself a happy or unhappy ending. Mrs Spark's fiction, where apparently trivial or irrelevant threads of narrative finally emerge, knit triumphantly together, as necessary to the structure of the whole, parallels this. Her art is the calculated equivalent of her religious beliefs: it postulates a scheme of things in which nothing is wasted. It is extremely economic, and, as Sandy Stranger tells herself in *The Prime of Miss Jean Brodie* (1961), 'it always seemed . . . that where there was a choice of various courses the most economical was the best'.[37]

One of the reasons why Mrs Spark would endorse this is because the procedure acts as a reminder of divine economy: though it is, as she recognizes too, only a reminder. Obviously, there are marked differences between art and life: and one of them is that, whereas the structure and purpose of a work of art are easily discernible, life itself is more obscure, lacks evident wholeness, is problematical, and fights against the imposition of a pattern—as Charmian Piper, one of Mrs Spark's many writer-figures, says, 'In life . . . everything is different.'[38] In the human sphere, people perceive truths and connections only dimly, tentatively—rather as Caroline Rose in *The Comforters* (1957) has occasional intimations of the novel being written round her, senses that this is happening, but is unable to discern the total pattern, the way in which events will mesh conclusively together. And often, too, there can be misinterpretation, farcical or serious misreading of existence's text: this Mrs Spark illustrates in *The Bachelors* (1960), where Alice Dawes decides she will believe in God if her lover, Patrick Seton, is acquitted of charges of fraudulent conversion being brought against him. In the event, he is convicted; sitting watching in the courtroom, ' "I don't believe in God," said Alice'[39]: what she does not know is that Seton was intending, if released, to murder her and the child she is expecting. Life, where everything seems muddled and confused and where people, unlike the characters of fiction, have free will, is to this extent the opposite of art, the province of order and necessity. Still, as a Catholic, Mrs Spark believes that, no matter how shapeless, how absurd, life may appear, this is only appearance, only the result of human inability to comprehend; the chaos is illusory; the apparently contingent is not really so; there is ultimately a significance. And by making some attempt to bring this out, even on a small scale, by showing that there is a purpose, an informing principle, behind the worlds on which she focuses attention in her novels—'glimpses that seem like a microcosm of reality'[40]—her art implies that there can be, too, behind the flux of life, some grand design. This is why she can think of it as 'fiction out of which a kind of truth emerges,'[41] why, though technically untrue, it is—nevertheless—a very moral type of lying.

It would, however, be misleading to imply that, because of this interpretation placed on their technique, these are books that stay opaque to pagan or agnostic eyes, private works of specialized appeal, relevant only to the theologically initiated, novels that to non-believers are eccentric tracts, quaint or offensive according to taste. Mrs Spark is not merely 'speaking from that Catholic point of view that takes some getting used to.'[42] There are, as her novels have increasingly displayed, very considerable aesthetic benefits to be derived from concentration of the type she practises. And, in any case, the enjoyment of elaborately ordered fiction, tense coherences, is far from limited to those who share Mrs Spark's theology. Indeed, it could be argued that, whilst the shapeliness of this kind of writing can appeal to a Catholic such as Mrs Spark because it accords with her view of life, it can appeal to the atheist or agnostic just as strongly on the converse grounds that it is the opposite of his—art here satisfying temporarily that human appetite for shape and neatness that a religion can permanently satisfy. Nor is it much to the point in this context to bring forward the charge that neatness and symmetry in art are dangerous qualities, that they can act as drugs, formal bromides, offering false consolation to those immersed in life's unavoidably painful and bewildering chaos. The fiction of Mrs Spark hands out no facile comforts. Though the form of her books is deeply satisfying—the gradual perception of parallels and patterns, echoing situations and new aptnesses, is one of the great pleasures to be experienced in reading them—there is, as counterpoint to this, the disturbing tenor of their content. Mrs Spark is invariably entertaining: there is nothing lifeless, bleakly didactic, nothing homiletic about her novels. 'I only claim credit for what I do with my ideas,'[43] she has said: and in her fiction she does a great deal. Her themes are always beautifully displayed: unerringly the various constituents of each book are pulled into graceful liaison, while the prose, kept continually crisp with irony, is equally capable of opening out into ordered paragraphs or contracting to some sharp, new phrase that hooks itself into the memory. The novels are attractive; they offer the relief of order: but they are not conducive to complacency. The facts to which they insistently return— that men are lonely, divided, prone to deceit and treachery, die and do not want to—are hardly comfortable. This fiction is tensing, astringent, aimed always at toning the muscles of discrimination, galvanizing alertness and self-scrutiny into a fiercer life, preventing the lazy mind and torpid moral sense from lapsing into dangerous sloth, scarcely evaluated patterns of behaviour, relaxed standards, sloppy half-beliefs. These books may be elegant, but they are elegant disturbers.

2

Islands

Probably the most noticeable thing about Muriel Spark's first novel, *The Comforters*, is that one of the characters in it knows she is a character, that Caroline Rose hears intermittently the book being written round her, comments critically upon it, and attempts to sabotage the structure—'I intend to stand aside and see if the novel has any real form apart from this artificial plot. I happen to be a Christian' (p.117).[1] Provoking talk of Chinese boxes and novels about The Novel, this aspect of the work has tended to attract the most attention, which is unfortunate, since the device here used, though locally amusing and ingenious, is finally of not much more than marginal importance. In fact, the book seems more rewardingly approached by following the pointer in its name: *The Comforters*. This is a reference to the Book of Job, a work which seems to have held Mrs Spark's attention for some time before she began writing her novels. In 1953, for instance, according to notes to an anthology containing one of her very early short stories, 'Harper and Wilton', she was 'at present working on a book on the Book of Job'.[2] The full-length study suggested here never appeared: but, in April 1955, the year in which she began to write *The Comforters*, an article on this subject by Mrs Spark was published in the *Church of England Newspaper*. It was called 'The Mystery of Job's Suffering', and several of its observations have an especial relevance to the novel then being written. In the article, Mrs Spark says of Job that 'He not only argues the problem of suffering, he suffers the problem of argument'[3]: and it is upon this interpretation of the work, seeing it as the portrayal of a man irritated almost beyond endurance by the misunderstanding of those around him, that she places her stress. Job, she writes, is 'surrounded by a conspiracy of mediocrity, obsessed with a raging need to shock them [the Comforters] and at the same time to communicate his feelings'[4]; she points to 'the complacent sentiments by which the Comforters take their several stands'[5]; and states that, as these people are insulated in very separate modes of thought, 'the dialogue makes no rational progress . . . the characters cannot understand each other'.[6] In her novel, which contains one brief explicit reference to the Book of Job (p.111), but is otherwise related to it only implicitly, Mrs Spark elaborates this situation. The role of the central sufferer is diminished— though Caroline does think at one point of 'her isolation by ordeal' (p.112), not very much is made of this—and the number of Comforters, of people who have difficulty in making contact with their fellows because they are locked behind the barriers of some very solipsistic mental world, is considerably increased.

The plot, a complex one, is mainly developed by means of the two chief characters, Laurence Manders and his ex-mistress, Caroline. Between them, they share important attributes of a novelist. Laurence, a compulsive investigator— he says of himself, 'I notice extraordinary things. . . . Things which people think are concealed' (p.13)—pries like a novelist into other lives. He is, however, 'not a wonderer' (p.14), cannot make satisfactory sense of what he finds, and depends for this on Caroline—'he felt the need of her co-ordinating mind to piece together the mysterious facts' (p.83)—a student and critic of fictional form, professionally knowledgeable about the ways in which life's raw material can be shaped and organized. Together, they encounter a great deal. Laurence's grandmother, Louisa Jepp, is, it emerges, engaged with a small gang in diamond smuggling. His mother, Helena, dangerously comp-licates life by her charitable efforts towards a former servant, the repulsive Mrs Hogg. Caroline begins to hear voices and to claim she is being written into a book. There is talk of the Black Mass, witches, and Satanic ritual. Bigamy and blackmail come to light. There is a violent death and, perhaps, a miracle. Deliberately and mockingly, the author complicates her 'artificial plot'—a baroque knot of grotesque incident, elab-orate interweavings, and extreme coincidence—until it almost seems a parody: it is, to the literary Caroline, like something from 'a cheap mystery piece' (p.115). What gives the book 'real form', its genuine unity, is that the characters are all Comforters, all isolated mentally, each inhabiting a private world of fantasy or of obsession that is remote and often inaccessible to others.

Caroline is the extreme example of this. Working on a book

dealing with 'Form in the Modern Novel' (p.59), she becomes convinced that she herself is being worked into a piece of fiction. What she laughingly says of Willi Stock, the excited observer of diabolism—' "He thinks he is aloof from the subject . . . merely inter-ested. Whereas he is passionately attracted to it. My nature," she quoted, "is subdued to what it works in, like the dyer's hand. Pity me then . . ." ' (p.218)—seems to rebound upon herself. Laurence, attempting to cope with her apparent delusion, suggests that what is happening is a kind of occupational disease, but Caroline refuses to accept what he is saying. She is aware, however, that between the two of them, already set dangerously apart by her recent conversion to Catholicism, a gulf is widening, and tries hard to lessen this: ' "Will you be able to make an occasional concession to the logic of my madness?" she asked him. "Because that will be necessary between us. Otherwise, we shall be really separated." She was terrified of being entirely separated from Laurence' (p.107). He agrees: but, less than a couple of hours later, Caroline beginning to interfere with his plans, is irritably asking himself, 'Why the hell should we be enslaved by her secret fantasy?' (p.108). With difficulty, the two do keep together: but only by making allowance for each other's differing *idées fixes*, not because of any mutual understanding. They do not enter each other's mental worlds: they simply respect them.

This is the burden of the book: that, intellectually, the individual is very much alone. When Willi Stock, obsessed by his researches into Satanism, finding absurd evidence for it everywhere—so that even Eleanor's vacuous plaint, 'Mrs. Hogg is a *witch*!' (p.165), rings in his fixated mind as literal truth—says to Caroline, 'I don't know really why I continue to open my mind to you' (p.204), the effect is one of utter irony. No one it seems from this book, is able to open his mind fully and confidently to another. Sooner or later, he will meet with incomprehension, if not betrayal. The world that each inhabits is too private to allow any real dialogue: and to emphasize this fact the author gives us in her characters a colourful anthology of mental eccentricity. Caroline detects signs of a novel being written everywhere around her, just as Willi continually finds further dubious proof—'people with obsessions could usually find evidence to fit their craziest convictions' (p.104)—for his beliefs about the Black Mass. With magpie single-mindedness, Laurence obsessively gathers data he can make no use of. Louisa's life centres contentedly around her smuggling escapades. Helena has shut herself into a sunshine world of baseless optimism and ill-considered charity, comfortably misinterpreting the actions of others so she can keep at bay the harsh realities. Eleanor vapidly acts out a repertoire of hackneyed fantasies, posturing and dramatizing to a degree where her own character has become invisible and almost nonexistent. Edwin Manders lives on religion as though it were a drug. Georgina Hogg thrives on perverted religiosity. Her husband, who has 'the decided air of one manqué' (p.23), draws nourishment from his private and self-pitying myth of lavish talent tragically frustrated by undeserved misfortune. To Caroline's question—'Is the world a lunatic asylum then? Are we all courteous maniacs discreetly making allowances for everyone else's derangement?' (p.204)—the novel offers a definite, if an amused, affirmative. Leading mental lives of such marked idiosyncrasy, lives coloured by their differing needs and personalities, these characters can achieve little in the way of mutual contact or of understanding. For the most part they remain comically incommunicado.

Nor is their isolation merely intellectual: they also tend to be emotionally and physically alone. Laurence and Caroline, once lovers, are now separated by her new religious scruples. Helena and Edwin are kept apart by his unworldliness. Mrs Jepp is a widow, though she does have an admirer whom she finally marries, thus contributing a mock conventional happy ending to the book. The homosexual Ernest has, 'for comfort's sake' (p.88), abandoned even casual affairs with men. Georgina Hogg is separated from her husband; so is Eleanor: he is, events reveal, the same husband. For all the wit bestowed on it, the world presented in this novel is a rather sombre one—a world in which people can eventually rely only upon themselves and their own resources, most kinds of love or union proving to be illusory, transient, or precarious. The Comforters here are no more able to offer consolation than they were in the Book of Job. The name is wry and ironic.

Structurally, *The Comforters* fails, not surprisingly in a first novel, to display that tight and total concentration later so typical of Mrs. Spark. It does, however, show her working towards it. In this book, she is, to a large extent, concerned with two communities: the world of the metropolitan fringe-intellectual, and that of the Catholic and the Catholic convert. Caroline, member of both, seeing one through disillusion's jaded eyes and the other with sardonic freshness, acts as linking figure. The first society—the preserve of what in *Robinson* are called 'intelligent loafers,'[7] the vaguely artistic *flâneur* and literary parasite—is, we are told, 'one of the half-worlds of Caroline's past, of which she had gradually taken leave; it was a society which she had half-forgotten, and of which she had come wholly to disapprove' (p.48). Her panic-stricken flight to Willi Stock, however, after the first onslaught of her voices, involves her of necessity in some return to it: for he—owner of 'a bookshop in Charing Cross Road, one of those which keep themselves exclusively intellectual. "Intellect-u-al," the Baron pronounced it' (p.49)—is both characteristic product of, and self-congratulatory spokesman for, this social group. They are, he says fondly, 'all a little mad and, my dear Caroline, that's what makes us so nice.' (pp.56–7). This is the aspect of the Bohemian half-world spotlit in *The Comforters*: the way in which its members preen themselves on mental quirks and aberrations, fondle their 'neuroses' and their oddities as marks of some distinction. These are Comforters infatuated with their isolating idiosyncrasies. And isolation is a keynote of their group. There are recognizable external features, insignia of the clan, most notably the inane argot, 'the dreary imprecise language of this half-world' (p.87), which Mrs Spark captures with her deft parodic flair:

> 'But you know,' said the girl, 'there's another side to Willi Stock. He's an orgiast on the quiet.'
> 'A what?'
> 'Goes in for the Black Mass. He's a Satanist. Probably that's why Eleanor left him. She's so awfully bourgeois' (p.87).

There are the outward signs of community and belonging—Caroline can think of her time as member of this group as one when neurosis 'was merely the badge of her tribe' (p.65)—but, behind them is no genuine *rapport*. The evening's drinking with Laurence, Ernest and Eleanor—an evening which provokes Caroline to remark, 'we've reached the stage where each one discourses upon his private obsession, regardless' (p.100)—is merely a reductio ad absurdum of what has already been much in evidence. Different thought-habits hold the characters apart, ensure that between them there is little communication. A collection of mental isolates kept only superficially together by tacit conformity to some shared social code, they stand as comically exaggerated microcosm, provide a ludicrous and an appropriate image for the novel's theme.

Importantly, too, theirs is a world in which there is, behind the surface camaraderie, no real warmth or loyalty, but on the contrary a continual need for caution, since in this circle the indiscreet confidence almost inevitably paves the way to spiteful or casual betrayal. Gossip and malicious chatter are rife among this empty confraternity, as Mrs Spark insistently reminds: 'Caroline collected, one way and another, that the Baron had been mentioning this and that about her, to the ageless boys and girls who dropped in on him at his bookshop in Charing Cross Road' (p.85); 'He told her a story in strictest confidence which, however, she repeated to Laurence before the day was out' (p.185).

This is the world that Caroline has left behind her. The one she has newly entered, through her conversion to Catholicism is equally disturbing, though for rather different reasons. If the emphasis in the society of Willi Stock and his circle was on ostentatious individuality, here it is upon conformity, community, love of one's fellows and the surrendering of personal inclination to the dictates of authority. It is obviously a society in which Caroline, with 'her private neurotic amusement' (p.30), can only exist uneasily. As Mrs Hogg, diametrically opposed to her, declares: 'You're the sort that doesn't mix. Catholics are very good mixers' (pp.29–30). Caroline herself is only too aware of this, reacts with fear to 'the terrifying collective' (p.111) and with revulsion to the spectacle of her religious-fellows at their 'morbid communal pleasures' (p.39), picking over memories of imagined slight and persecution. The lack of privacy, the limiting of individual scope oppress her. Her brief stay, in the hope of contemplation and recovery from her nervous trouble, at the Pilgrim Centre of St Philumena acts as sharp reminder that 'the popular meaning of "retreat" in religious circles was an organized affair, not a private retiring from customary activities, so as to possess one's soul in peace' (p.30). In this community, too marked an individuality is suspect and difficult to maintain. Pacing the corridors alone in search of privacy, Caroline is quickly joined by Mrs Hogg and: 'The small perfect idea which had been crystallizing in her mind went all to mist. All right; I am at your disposal. Eat me, bloody well take the lot. I am feeling lonely. Rome has spoken' (p.27). Mrs Hogg, from whom Caroline has, in the end, literally to beat her way free, epitomizes, it soon emerges, the menace of this way of life. Representing everything that is most loathsome in communal existence—alone, we are ironically informed, she simply vanishes because, she 'is not all there' (p.175)—and manifesting in extreme and perverse form the anti-individualistic tendency of Catholicism, she stands, too, as a parody of charitable concern. Her interest in her neighbour, compulsive, relentlessly attentive, is that of the spy and psychological blackmailer. And through her Mrs Spark calls in question the whole Christian insistence upon charity:

> the memory of mealtimes at St. Philumena's returned, with the sight of Mrs. Hogg chewing in rhythm with the reading from the Scriptures delivered in the Sister's refined modulations: 'Beloved, let us love one another, love springs from God. . . . If a man boasts of loving God, while he hates his own brother, he is a liar . . . the man who loves God must be one who loves his brother.' . . .
> Caroline thought, 'The demands of the Christian religion are exorbitant, they are outrageous. Christians who don't realize that from the start are not faithful. They are dishonest; their teachers are talking in their sleep. "Love one another . . . brethren, beloved . . . your brother, neighbours, love, love, love"—do they know what they are saying'?
> She stopped eating, was conscious of two things, a splitting headache and Mrs. Hogg. These bemused patterers on the theme of love, had they faced Mrs. Hogg in person? (pp. 37–8).

Clarity, Mrs Spark insists, must come before charity. Nebulous urges towards philanthropy must not get in the way of truth: which, of all the virtues, is that she rates most highly. It has 'airy properties with buoyant and lyrical effects,'[8] the narrator of one short story tells herself, whilst the heroine of another comes to realize: 'There is no health for me outside of honesty.'[9] The approval given to Harry Clegg, the archaeologist in *The Mandelbaum Gate*, because 'He would not, for the love of Barbara or anyone else, attribute a date which he knew to be false to a manuscript or object of antiquity'[10] is characteristic: as is the moment in 'Bang-Bang You're Dead', where Mrs Spark, watching her protagonist cynically endorsing inauthentic chatter, warningly remarks, 'She did not then know that the price of allowing false opinions was the gradual loss of one's capacity for forming true ones.'[11] It is necessary, she always emphasizes, to see and define facts and people plainly, free from any sentimental blurring. The precision and clarity of her prose style are the equivalents of those qualities she considers essential to any healthy moral or intellectual life. Things must be recognized for what they are: and one of the most important things to be so recognized is human fallibility. 'We should know ourselves better by now,' she has said, 'than to be under the illusion that we are all essentially aspiring, affectionate, and loving creatures. We do have these qualities, but we are aggressive too.'[12] This is a consideration with which truth must come to terms, a factor which must play its part in any meaningful concept of charity. Unguarded trust in the goodness of others—something which, as Mrs Spark sees it, often loosely passes for charity (and Helena in *The Comforters* is a sardonically noted instance of this)—is, in view of man's vicious potentialities, at best, foolish, and, at worst, extremely dangerous. An abstention from aggression but with defensive weapons close at hand, a kind of armed tolerance, is the usual social stance of Mrs Spark's central characters: and, given the behaviour depicted in her novels, this appears necessary.

The fictional world of this author is one in which there is little easy warmth or relaxation, but, rather, a continual need for vigilance since people are rarely what they seem. That the human being is not to be trusted is, for Mrs Spark, a social paradigm—one conjugated in her fiction through treachery and blackmail ('Life is based on blackmail,'[13] says a character in *Robinson*, and certainly, in one form or another, it occurs in almost all these books) to violence and the occasional murder. Instances of modern man's mortal and venial inhumanities to man pervade her works, with larger-scale harshnesses colouring the background of the three books that look to more political

24

concerns: *The Prime of Miss Jean Brodie, The Girls of Slender Means,* and *The Mandelbaum Gate.* In this atmosphere, conversations are almost always edgy and cautious, verbal thrust being repaid if possible and almost as routine—the sight of the other cheek being turned is rare in this fiction—by careful counter-thrust. And this is not only between enemies: it applies equally to those who genuinely like each other, as when Laurence, in *The Comforters,* ignorant of her real reasons, rather patronizingly teases his grandmother about her plan to buy a boat, should she win a fortune on the football pools:

'A yacht? Oh, how grand.'
'Well, a good-sized boat,' said Louisa, 'that's what I'd buy. Suitable for crossing the Channel.'
'A motor-cruiser,' Laurence suggested.
'That's about it,' she said.
'Oh, how grand.'
She did not reply, for he had gone too far with his 'Oh, how grand!'
'We could do the Mediterranean,' he said.
'Oh, how grand,' she said' (p.8).

Small scratches of this kind are constantly being inflicted in Mrs Spark's fiction. No relationship is to be taken on trust. There is continual need for the individual to assert himself socially, to show that he is not to be intimidated by the condescensions or aggressions of others. Benevolence, in this context, is usually interpreted as weakness and responded to accordingly—as in the case of well-intentioned, woolly-minded Helena, with her refrain, 'One tries to be charitable' (pp. 77, 208, 210), and the repeated rebuffs she meets with in the course of her blinkered philanthropy. Frequently, in *The Comforters,* she makes an effort to help Mrs Hogg; always, there is some unpleasant backlash. Finally, strongly driving home her point, Mrs Spark shows Helena cajoling Caroline—'This really is charitable' (p.224)—to aid the woman, too: with the result that Caroline is nearly drowned, dragged to the bottom of the Thames by Mrs Hogg's unyielding clutch.

Mrs Spark's view of life may be harsh but it is scrupulously honest. She can speak, for instance, of the way Caroline 'was almost shocked to find how she seemed to derive composure from the evidence of her friend's dissolution' (p.96)—and the

modifying adverb is typical. This is a writer to whom senti-
mentality is alien, aware that truth can be disturbing, hostile
to the cosy and protective myths which people use to blunt the
edge of life's sharper facts: and she is not reluctant to peel away
these myths. Charity, love, loyalty, concepts such as these
undergo a stringent reassessment in her fiction and are sharply
redefined. Insisting on the value of the real thing—and in
works such as *The Mandelbaum Gate* or *The Public Image* (1968)
love becomes a central and redemptive force—Mrs Spark
rejects the numerous spurious substitutes for it, discriminates,
points to, and is contemptuous of, the inauthentic in the interests
of the genuine. 'Don't you think you misconstrue charity?'
(p.210) Caroline asks Helena at one stage of *The Comforters*.
The author shows she does, and, in her other books, that there
are many like her.

Caroline, of course, 'sharp, inquiring . . . grisly about the
truth' (pp.32-3), is a type that recurs throughout this fiction.
Gifted, like Barbara Vaughan of *The Mandelbaum Gate*, 'with an
honest analytical intelligence, a sense of fidelity in the observing
of observable things,'[14] clear-sighted enough to be exasperated
at human absurdity and candid enough to recognize that the
demands of universal love urged on her by her Catholic
religion are unrealistic, she looks for salvation through the
intellect rather than the emotions. It is in faith, not charity,
that she places her hope. She is religious, but, as Edwin
Manders points out, religious in a peculiar sense: 'Very little
heart for it, all mind' (p.231)—similar, in fact, to the persona
of one of Mrs Spark's poems, who confesses:

> I by Faith am much imbued
> And can't be bothered with my Neighbour.[15]

Charity is something that comes hard to Caroline. It is rarely
spontaneous, but achieved rather, as with Ronald Bridges in
The Bachelors, by deliberately 'making some effort of will
towards graciousness'.[16] Like many Spark protagonists, she is
torn between the firm belief that people are important, that
their actions have an eternal significance, and an equally
strong distaste for their inadequacy: petty aggressions and
disruptions, complacent immersion in trivia.

Caroline is also, it is noticeable, in many ways like Mrs
Spark herself, her background having much in common with

the author's own. She has, we are told, spent some time in Africa, lived by writing free-lance criticism, is of partly Jewish descent, and has become converted to Catholicism. All these are equally true of Mrs Spark. And there is an interesting passage, too, where Caroline remembers 'a time when her brain was like a Guy Fawkes night, ideas cracking off in all directions, dark idiot-figures jumping round a fiery junk-heap in the centre' (p.34). Again, this comes close to something in Mrs Spark's own experience. 'The first reaction I had when I became a Catholic,' she has said, 'was that my mind was far too crowded with ideas, all teeming in disorder . . .'.[17] Before her conversion, she had experienced a writer's block—'I had written nothing for over a year'[18] and 'I wasn't able to work and to do any of my writing until I became a Catholic'[19]: then, 'suddenly,' she said, 'I found I could write, things were taking shape as if there had been a complete reorganization of my mind,'[20] and 'When I got my ideas under control . . . it coincided with the time I was beginning to get better and with my conversion'.[21]

It was, this indicates, the philosophy rather than the moral programme of the Catholic Church that first attracted Mrs Spark: and what drew her especially to this philosophy was that it offered a view of life in which there is no waste, in which everything, no matter how contingent it appears, is ultimately part of a coherent whole, subject finally to a controlling force. In this, of course, it bears a close relation to her fictional technique, something of which she is herself aware: 'I think there is a connection between my writing and my conversion,'[22] she has noted, and this connection is not simply, or even primarily, a matter of moral attitude. Though the ethics of Mrs Spark's Catholicism do provide some of the positives from which her satire works—her religion is, she has said, 'a norm from which one can depart . . . something to measure from'[23]— it is the philosophy, with its concept of life as an economy of meaningful structure, that is of the real importance to her as an artist. What is said in *The Comforters* to Louisa Jepp applies with greater aptness to the author herself: 'You can't bear to participate in separated worlds. You have the instinct for unity, for coordinating the inconsistent elements of experience. You have the passion for picking up the idle phenomena of life and piecing them together' (p.18). She is a highly organizing, very economic novelist: and even here, in her first novel, this can be clearly seen. The plot of *The Comforters* may, to begin with, give the appearance of meandering, but this is a deliberate device and quickly shown to be illusory. Links and inter-relationships are constantly being forged; more and more connections are disclosed; seeming irrelevancies turn into essentials as new light is cast. Complex and elaborately rami-fied, the plot is made to prove that what appears fortuitous and casual is not really so but ultimately earns its keep, playing, sometimes surprisingly, its necessary part in the structure of the whole. And always, too, behind these careful convolutions of the narrative, there is, as further unifying element, the fact that all the characters portrayed are similar in kind, show symptoms of the same malaise, are mental isolates, blundering absurdly in a solipsistic haze, misunderstanding and misunderstood. Heavily plotted, peopled with a vivid, varied dramatis personae, the book is still distinguished by a fairly strict thematic unity. In it, Mrs Spark's impressive powers of control, the discipline and the selection that so stamp her art, are already notable. And in addition, other strengths can be seen emerging in this first novel. The author's satirical gifts, for instance, are in evidence here, especially in the scenes where she depicts eccentric en-claves of Catholic or Bohemian society, lightly but efficiently nailing down pretence and affectation:

> At the first pub, after they had left, a friend of Laurence had said, 'That's Larry's form of perversion—beautiful neurotic women. They have to be neurotic.'
> It was understood that every close association between two people was a perversion (p.84).

And there are, too, her stylistic talents—the freshening of a jaded phrase: 'Mrs. Hogg came out of hiding as if she had never been in it' (p.216); a slightly unexpected word used with satisfactory accuracy: 'Their new-found faith was expressed in a rowdy contempt for the Church of England' (p.38); obvious delight in heightened language ordered into syntax of some elegance: 'He was accustomed to Louisa's food: whelks, peri-winkles, milts and roes, chitterlings and sweetbreads, giblets, brains and the tripes of ruminating animals. Louisa prepared them at long ease, by many processes of affusion, diffusion and immersion, requiring many pans of brine, many purifications and simmerings, much sousing and sweetening by slow degrees' (pp. 7–8).

The Comforters has its weaknesses, which largely stem, perhaps, from the fact that it is a first novel and, on occasion, rather whimsically self-conscious about the conventions of the mode in which its author works. This comes out most clearly, of course, in the matter of Caroline and her voices, which is never really integrated into the book but remains a misleading excrescence. It is not so much that this material is fantastic (in *Memento Mori*, Mrs Spark shows what she can really do with fantasy) as that it is finally somewhat irrelevant, an attention-catching gimmick but not functional at all: and, as one of those things nourishing the fallacy that Mrs Spark is basically no more than a roguish purveyor of teasing trivialities, it is especially to be regretted. Despite this, however, *The Comforters* is a valuable start, in which the author's main preoccupations already appear and her fictional technique is developed to a degree where only more rigour and refinement are needed to put the formal triumphs of the later novels well within her grasp. Then, surprisingly, with her next book, she turned to something very different.

Robinson, a rather tantalizing and ambiguous work, is in several ways an odd man out amongst the books of Muriel Spark, unusual even in its narrative technique, this being the only one of her novels so far to be told in the first person. The narrator, however, is very recognizable. Catholic convert, 'poet, critic and general articulator of ideas' (p. 18),[24] January Marlow has immediate similarities with both Caroline Rose of *The Comforters* and Mrs Spark herself in the days before she started writing fiction. Close to Caroline in temperament, another self-reliant woman, January is even more detached and solitary: widowed now, in fact, after a very brief and ill-matched marriage. Hearing this and that she is a journalist, one of her companions remarks, 'Those are two conditions of life that make for resourcefulness' (p. 18): and events confirm his words. Again like Caroline, January is well able to hold her own, not a woman to be socially intimidated. Early in the book, indeed, flying out to the Azores to complete a literary assignment, she reflects complacently upon her expertise in handling situations:

I find that, when travelling abroad alone, it is wise and actually discreet to take up with one well-chosen man on the journey. Otherwise, one is likely to be approached by numerous chance pesterers all along the line. One must, of course, discriminate, but it is a thing one learns by experience, how to know the sort of man who is not likely to press for future commitments (pp.22–3).

But things do not go according to plan. Her plane crashes with only three survivors on to 'a tiny man-shaped Atlantic island' (p.185), owned by, and named after, a recluse called Robinson. And recounting the way in which these people—Robinson; January; her fellow-passengers, Tom Wells and Jimmie Waterford—react to their new life and to each other's close, continual proximity, the book presents itself, at first sight, as a sophisticated exercise in desert-island writing, its title acting as a reminder of those classic works, *Robinson Crusoe*, *The Swiss Family Robinson*, with which it shares its basic situation.

Most of the customary features of the castaway-survival genre are on duty in the book. Its physical setting is painted in great detail. The vegetation and terrain of Robinson, its cliffs and secret tunnels, snow-white beach and yellow mustard field, the lake and screaming furnace, these are described with painstaking accuracy. The book is even prefaced by a traditional map, making clear any complications of topography. Day-to-day events are patiently and scrupulously chronicled (much of the novel is supposed to derive from January's journal, and the whole narrative is far more expansive than is usual with Mrs Spark). We hear how the characters recover slowly from their injuries and shock; we see their lives shaping to a new routine; we are told of various jobs that must be undertaken, watch the efforts made to fend off boredom—record-evenings, ping-pong sessions with the cat, games with Robinson's young protégé, Miguel. Yet, for all this documentary display, all its journalistic detail, the book is not simply an adventure tale, not merely an enlarged, superior version of Wells's newspaper article, with its exclamatory questions: 'What's it like to be an island castaway? To come face to face with the Alone? ... To endure the agony of loneliness, knowing that the folks at home have given up hope?', and its stirring claim: '*I never knew what true comradeship was till I lived on that island*' (p.180).

There is, to begin with, very little of this comradeship displayed. Contrary to the conventions, this is a Robinson eager to preserve his solitude. '*Nunquam minus solus quam cum solus*' (p.21) is his motto: never less alone than when alone. These are survivors uneasy and even hostile in one another's company. Flung together on the island, they are received with only reluctant hospitality by its owner, and form at best a nervy and precarious community. Far from banding together into thankful companionship against the threat of the unknown, they view each other, through long days of convalescence and monotony, with dislike and irritation. There are petty rivalries; quarrels flare; alliances are brief and shaky, never permanent. Robinson's departure, amidst spectacular, blood-stained, and murder-indicating circumstances, exacerbates already fierce tension, drives the others even deeper into suspicion and isolation. Finally, the latent violence, coming to the surface in the form of brawls and pistol shots, is nearly fatal.

Then, too, there is the fact that what Wells calls 'the folks at home' are not entirely absent from the island: out of sight, perhaps, but far from out of mind. Marooned as she is, January soon finds two of her fellow-castaways oddly reminiscent of her relatives. 'Robinson,' she says, 'resembled in appearance, my brother-in-law, Ian Brodie. . . . It was not a strong resemblance—a matter only of the shape of the head, but I wished that it did not exist, seeing that I should have to live with Robinson till August' (p.19); again she notes, 'Tom Wells bore a strong resemblance to my brother-in-law, the bookie, Curly Lonsdale' (p.53): and, as she comes to know the two men better, these resemblances prove to go beyond the purely physical. Robinson, it emerges, does not only look like Brodie: he also shares with him noticeable traits of character. Both are cold men, critical and prone to domineer; both, for all their paraded self-control, capable of acting with disturbing violence: Robinson disappears, leaving behind him clothes daubed in the blood of the slaughtered goat; Brodie's idea of a joke is to telephone a man, announcing that his wife has cancer. Both, too, are contemptuous of women; both, Catholics appalled at the spread of Marian devotion. At least, Robinson had originally been Catholic. Reacting against what he regards as dangerous idolatry, he has since detached himself from the church. Brodie, on the other hand, inveighing in safe privacy against these same 'abuses', cautiously retains his membership. The resemblances between the two men, as this indicates, though marked, are far from total. Robinson is much more sympathetic, 'far more intelligent and more controlled' (p.82), as January says. What in him are slightly troubling or briefly unpleasant traits appear in Brodie grossly magnified. Robinson is indifferent to women: Brodie is impotent; Robinson rationally scrutinizes Marian doctrine: Brodie shrilly denounces it; Robinson behaves badly on occasion: Brodie does so consistently. What Brodie represents, in fact, is the repulsive extreme, almost a caricature, of Robinson's type of personality, a man in whom the other's flaws and vices, heightened and hardened, stand out with ugly clarity.

In the case of Wells and Lonsdale, the situation is similar, but, this time, in reverse. Here, it is the man on the island who stands as vicious exaggeration of the other's character. Curly Lonsdale, raffish, vulgar, moving in a loud milieu of smashers, snifters, and racing bets, is not to January's taste, but he is, she recognizes, far less reprehensible than Wells, whose psychic magazine and attendant flummery act as a useful front for a remunerative industry in blackmail and pornography. Still, the two men do show similarities and both stand at the opposite extreme to Robinson and Brodie: versions of the id-dominated personality set, in contrast, against two treatments of the super-ego type. And this polarity is further strengthened by the fact that, in marrying, Brodie and Lonsdale have each chosen a partner from their own character group—Agnes, Brodie's wife, sharing his brand of puritanical nastiness; Julia, Lonsdale's wife, her husband's irresponsibility. In addition, extending the cat's cradle even further, these two women are January's sisters, and, though she is now estranged from them, there are, as she reminds herself, fugitive moments of affinity:

I . . . settled down to the interesting thought of how like I was at this moment to my sister Julia. There is something about too much worry that brings out Julia in me, a temporary reaction which is typical of her constant behaviour. . . . And I mused on other occasions of special stress when on the other hand, I was Agnes to the life. . . . My hangover, perhaps a kind of protection against excitability, took the form of a fat-headed domestic triviality. . . . This would last but a few hours, but Agnes did it all her life (pp.160–1).

Transient likenesses of this kind are continually remarked on in the book. Even the situation of Miguel, surrounded by adults competing for his interest, is for January reminiscent of her son, Brian, and the position he will now be in. And besides these constant reminders of life outside the island, similarities are indicated, too, between those wrecked upon it. January feels that 'Jimmie looks slightly like Robinson, about the nose' (p.16): and he proves to be related to him. Wells and Jimmie, mutually antagonistic, still have moments of resemblance: 'I felt that in opposing Jimmie and Wells I was up against two different types of the melodramatic mind,' January says, 'one coloured by romance, the other by crime' (p.152). She herself is at times like Robinson, speaking of 'the fear of over-familiarity which I shared with him' (p.52): and, when she shows a taste for cabaret, is even told by Wells, 'My word... we've got a lot in common, you and I' (p.47).

Interestingly, too, the people on the island all have one more marked peculiarity in common, the fact that their surnames are also the names of places—something quite purposefully stressed:

'Where am I?'
'Robinson,' he said.
'*Where*?'
'Robinson'. . . .
'Who are you?'
'Robinson,' he said. 'How do you feel?'
'*Who*?'
'Robinson' (p.5);

and:

'What is your name?' he said.
'January Marlow.'
'Think,' he said. 'Try to think.'
'Think of what?'
'Your name.'
'January Marlow,' I said, and placed the mug of soup on the floor beside me. He lifted the mug and replaced it in my right hand.

'Sip it, and meanwhile think. You have told me the month and place of your birth. What is your name?'

'I was rather pleased about his mistake' (p.6);

and:

> Robinson said: 'You must have heard it from Waterford.'
> 'I've never been to Waterford.'
> 'Jimmie Waterford,' he said (p.15);

and, with rather less overtness: ' "This is Ethel of the Well", said Tom Wells. . . . "The original Ethel," said Wells, "was found in a well in Somerset." ' (pp.54–5). In keeping with all this, just as the island on which the events take place is shaped like a man, a fact which receives some emphasis, so the characters themselves are sometimes spoken of in terms borrowed from geography. Thinking of her sisters, for instance, January talks of 'the only common ground between us—our childhood' (p.11); we hear that, among some of the characters, 'the decent gulfs did not last' (p.45); that January, Wells, and Jimmie 'were on the same island but in different worlds' (p.152): and the idea lurking in all this comes out into the light when, answering Jimmie's quotation, 'No man is an island' (p.17), January says, 'Some are. . . . Their only ground of meeting is concealed under the sea. If words mean anything, and islands exist, then some people are islands' (p.18).

Not only is topography, in this book, often thought of in human terms—the island having arms and legs, a knee and headlands—but, conversely, people are thought of in terms of topography. As in Matthew Arnold's poem, 'To Marguerite',[25] these are characters who find themselves 'in the sea of life enisl'd': yet it is not just a case of 'echoing straits' and 'unplumb'd, salt, estranging sea' stretching divisively between them. There are also, it is pointed out, subterranean connections, things held surprisingly in common by the most unlikely people. 'I have seen a bus conductor who resembles a woman don of my acquaintance,' January says, 'I have seen the face of Agnes throwing itself from side to side in the pulpit' (p.144). Elaborating the idea lightly touched on here, mapping a whole network of resemblances between its characters, *Robinson* provides a kind of annexe to *The Comforters*. Both are books concerned with isolation, but, in the second, the emphasis falls more upon the odd connections that, despite this, can exist. 'Human nature,' it suggests, 'does not vary very much'(p.175); the individual may be basically alone, it grants: but then goes on to show the unexpected ways, some shared feature of physique or character, in which he can be also very like his fellows, linked obliquely but quite firmly to them. 'I'm rather interested in islands' (p.25), says January, the author's alter ego: and, after *The Comforters*, a book concerned with intellectual isolation, *Robinson* offers the conceit of island-like people cast together on an island that is like a person, characters never satisfactorily united nor ever fully independent, members one of another and socially abrasive.

This is the central theme of the book, but there are others too. There seems, for instance, to be some attempt to sketch out a distinction between male and female attitudes to life: that of the male is presented as predominantly rational, concerned with what can be proved or logically argued, whereas the female—'it is said the pagan mind runs strong in women at any time' (p.3)—owes more to instinct. This is most significant in the clash between January and Robinson over the rosary: something which she values and he detests because, she says, he is 'constitutionally afraid of any material manifestation of Grace' (p.103). This is a revealing statement, one which indicates the closeness of this book, as of all Mrs Spark's fiction, to her essay on Proust, 'The Religion of an Agnostic'. In that piece, speaking of 'the tendency to equate matter with evil,'[26] she stressed the need to return to what she called 'a sacramental view of life which is nothing more than a balanced regard for matter and spirit,'[27] a view of life which accepts that grace can—and does—exist under material aspects. Without being aware of the religious implications of his ideas, Proust, she feels, is teaching something similar. For him, some chance material stimulus like the crumb of madeleine can unlock a hoard of memory and, by short-circuiting across it, offer redemption from time or 'a way of apprehending eternity through our senses analogous to our sacramental understanding of eternity by faith'.[28] In *Robinson*, similar mechanics are seen at work: 'Sometimes I am a little vague about the details of the day before yesterday until some word or thing, almost a sacramental, touches my memory, and then the past comes walking over me as we say an angel is walking over our grave, and I stand in the past as in the beam of a searchlight' (p.2). According to Catholic doctrine, a sacramental is a material object, a rosary, holy water, which acts as aid to prayer and meditation, provides some kind of spiritual stimulus. For Mrs Spark, there is an equivalence between this and the process of memory noted by Proust. In both cases, a material object is triggering off something of metaphysical significance, the difference being that the action is voluntary in one instance and involuntary in the other—as she says, 'An involuntary act of remembrance, to Proust, is a suggestive shadow of what a voluntary act of remembrance is to a Christian'.[29] And the concept has important relevance to her own writings, too. Like sacramentals, the societies, the symbols and quasi-allegorical structures of her fiction are intended to stir the mind to contemplation, to make the reader aware of the existence, behind material aspects, of what she calls 'another world than this'.[30]

Somewhat oddly, though, for all its talk of sacramentals and material manifestations of grace, all its insistence on the island as 'a time and landscape of the mind' (p.1), *Robinson* finally shows itself to be the novel in which Mrs Spark's allegorical endeavour is least happy. Technically, in fact, the book veers even towards the crude. More than in any other of her works, the unity is here achieved by concentration of a purely physical kind, the limitation of the desert island, and, less than in any other, by the fact that the characters involved share some attribute, some common feature of their personality or situation. Normally in a book by Mrs Spark, the figures peopling the plot seem to be selected and then held in place by the thematic pull, chosen because of what they all exemplify. Here, they serve not much more than a narrative function. True, there is the emphasized web of resemblances, some trivial, some important, but the impression that this ultimately gives is of a rather arbitrary, mechanical contrivance. At once very neat and very unlikely, the geometry suggested—characters arranging themselves obligingly into categories—appears imposed rather than observed. To refer to the island as 'a place of the mind' is to invest it with more significance than it is capable of carrying with conviction. It is never shown to be so in the way that, say, the Jerusalem of *The Mandelbaum Gate* is both a graphic depiction of the mid-twentieth-century city and also the symbolic embodiment of the novel's theme. In

Robinson, the commonplace is not satisfactorily transfigured; the central situation retains the appearance of an extreme and local coincidence, not something of wider relevance; a convincing image is not created out of the society portrayed. The man-shaped island, which, at first sight, looks the most allegorical of all Mrs Spark's settings, turns out to be the least effectively so.

There is in *Robinson* a sense of content not fully subdued to an imaginative pattern, of a narrative either embroidered with arcane concurrences—the insistent trios, for example: January, one of three sisters, marooned with three men for three months after a plane crash in which there were just three survivors and which happened when she was flying out to research a work about three islands for 'a series which included books about threes of everything. Three rivers, three lakes, and threes of mountains, courtesans, battles, poets, old country houses'(p.78) —or allowed to remain casual and somewhat formless: so casual in fact, that, now and then, barely transmuted bits of personal material break jarringly through the fictive covering, sometimes in the form of rather ponderous private jokes. 'Muriel the Marvel with her X-ray eyes' (p.62) is a case in point. Appearing in the advertisement columns of Wells's magazine, *Your Future*, she is not hard to identify, particularly as she is nudgingly said to resemble Emily Brontë, about whom Mrs Spark had some years previously written a book in collaboration with Derek Stanford, presumably the 'Brother Derek' (p.62) of the same page. Self-conscious doodling of this type— which leads one to wonder if there may be some private code operating in other parts of the book as well: Mrs Spark has a son named Robin, and, besides the pat way the word Robinson breaks down, Brian is almost an anagram of this—suggests that the author, attempting a different kind of novel from her previous work, *The Comforters*, finds herself, among the book's looser, more journalistic conventions, uneasy and a little unsure. At any rate, she herself seems to have found the experiment unsatisfactory, for in her next book, *Memento Mori* (1959), she returned to the pattern established with *The Comforters*: a pattern which, since then, she has increasingly refined and tightened, stringently and more and more paring off irrelevance. The laxer blueprint used for *Robinson* has apparently been shelved.[31]

3
The Metropolitan City

Published in rapid succession—all three appeared between March 1959 and October 1960—*Memento Mori*, *The Ballad of Peckham Rye*, and *The Bachelors* together constitute a second phase in Muriel Spark's development as novelist. After those first books, *The Comforters* and *Robinson*, assured in many ways but still displaying signs of inexperience, still noticeably tentative about which fictional strategy to follow, Mrs Spark now shows herself in full control of her abilities and very certain as to how she wants to use them. Taking as general background to each book 'London, the metropolitan city,'[1] the author narrows in upon three different facets of it: a circle of moribund acquaintances, a working-class community, a coterie of bachelors. Then—rather like pitching a stone into a stagnant pond—some disruptive element is violently dispatched into this semi-closed community, the resulting turmoil —swirls and eddies, shifting sediment, glimpses of things normally submerged—wryly being noted and described: and, all the time, alongside this sardonic reportage, the little enclave is being carefully transformed by means of concentration, emphasis, selection into a powerful and memorable symbol.

Memento Mori was the first of the series to be published and, describing its genesis, Mrs Spark has said:

> I decided to write a book about old people. It happened that a number of old people I had known as a child in Edinburgh were dying from one cause or another, and on my visits to Edinburgh I sometimes accompanied my mother to see them in hospital. When I saw them I was impressed by the power and persistence of the human spirit. They were paralysed or crippled in body, yet were still exerting characteristic influences on those around them and in the world outside. I saw a tragic side to this situation and a comic side as well. I called this novel *Memento Mori*.[2]

This roughly maps the boundaries of the book's preserve—its great concern with age and death—but gives somewhat misleading emphasis to just one feature of it. Certainly the novel does depict the situation of weak flesh and willing spirit, of the enfeebled and malfunctioning body acting as a kind of obstacle round which the personality must painfully manoeuvre its intents and purposes: yet this is not in any way the linch-pin of the work. At that point, holding it together, there is not the tragi-comic spectacle of will pushing its way through the debilities of age, but, rather, the unsettling memorandum that gives the book its name.

As novelist, Muriel Spark has always shown a preference for the small community. In *Memento Mori*, that she concentrates upon is not merely limited; it is also shrinking, both literally and metaphorically: the former in that, as obituary columns fill with names of friends and relatives, the social circle of the old contemporaries portrayed continually contracts; the latter in that the minds of most anxiously recoil from the reason for this. To the anthem complaining in the background of this work, that classic plangency, *Timor mortis conturbat me*, many ears attempt determined deafness. And so the unwelcome, elementary truth, 'Remember you must die', is spread throughout the book by a device from fantasy. Taking the idea of the anonymous phone call, arbitrary harassment by dialled threats and warnings, Mrs Spark adapts this to her needs; pushes it to an extreme; turns it more or less to metaphor. The old people in her book are troubled by a caller who reminds them they must die. Theories about his identity busily proliferate; most are hopelessly misguided, merely casting light upon the fears and obsessions of the ageing minds in which they germinate, though one minor figure does unwittingly pin down the point at issue: ' "The question is," said Mr. Rose, "who's the fellow that's trying to put the fear of God in us?" ' (p.168).[3] Two characters, it seems—and they the novel's most intelligent —could offer him the answer. Henry Mortimer, a retired police officer called in to help with the case, unofficially explains, 'in my opinion the offender is Death himself' (p.157), a theory endorsed by Jean Taylor, Catholic, ex-companion to a novelist, and the character whose viewpoint comes closest to Mrs Spark's: ' "In my belief," she said, "the author of the anonymous telephone calls is Death himself, as you might say. . . . If you don't remember Death, Death reminds you to do so" ' (p.195).

To an extent, then, in that it allows a supernatural agency to needle at its characters, the book is fantasy. But its effect is far from one of whimsy. In her study of John Masefield, Mrs Spark noted 'how sharp and lucid fantasy can be when it is deliberately intagliated on the surface of realism'[4]: and this formula applies well to her own approach. In *Memento Mori*, the authorship of the calls is not, or should not be, the focus of interest. Death telephoning his reminders is simply the witty updating of a literary convention, a convenient, if baroque, way of transmitting those intimations of mortality with which the novel is concerned; the mysterious caller only puts into plain words a message already sounding, at one level or another, in the minds of all his hearers. What is important, what must be authentic, is the nature of response to the unpalatable fact broadcast so widely and disturbingly. 'It is surprising', says Charmian, this novel's novelist, 'how variously people react to the same thing' (p.206). The book in which she figures illustrates this plentifully.

The most common reaction is that established in the work's first scene, where Lettie Colston, having just received another death-reminder, complains to her brother that the speaker has used:

> 'Just the same words—*Remember you must die*—nothing more.'
> 'He must be a maniac,' said Godfrey (p.2).

In an obvious sense, of course, Godfrey's response is reasonable —anonymous callers do tend to be mentally disturbed—but, looked at from another angle, it neatly summarizes human unwillingness to face up to mortality. What the caller has announced, 'Remember you must die', is simple fact. To counter it with accusations of mania is to show a personal unbalance. But it is not in any way unusual. Godfrey's attitude is shared— carried, indeed, to the point of parody—by his sister Lettie, who, lowering her voice to speak of death, as she does when mentioning what she calls, 'the lavatory question' (p.32), refers to the 'terrible message' (p.106) as 'a troublesome remark' (p.35) and 'that distressing sentence' (p.35). Rather than accept a truth that undercuts the ego, she takes refuge in increasingly paranoid delusions; fleeing the idea of death, shuts herself away from life. Even more impervious to the

caller's message, though, is Mrs Pettigrew. While other characters erect elaborate structures of evasion, nervously attempt to
blame the criminal or lunatic, she ruthlessly suppresses the
disturbing words, forgets that she has ever had her warning:

> Mrs. Pettigrew, though she had in fact, one quiet after-
> noon, received the anonymous telephone call, had chosen to
> forget it. She possessed a strong faculty for simply refusing
> to admit an unpleasant situation, and going quite blank
> where it was concerned . . . it was not a plain ignoring of
> the incident; she omitted even to keep a mental record of it,
> but put down the receiver and blacked it out from her life
> (p.171).

Mrs Pettigrew, a blackmailer, is the most evil person in the
book, and her reaction is accordingly appropriate: for, in this
work, degrees of refusal to accept the chastening fact and
implications of mortality are made to stand in direct proportion
to differing degrees of moral corruption. And this means, of
course, that not all respond to the reminder with indignant fear
or self-induced hysteria. Just as descriptions of the caller's voice
widely vary, so do reactions to it. Some, for instance, who have
occupational means of handling new phenomena, find it
interesting. Percy Mannering, a poet, avidly seizes his experience and wrings from it:

> a Shakespearean sonnet entitled 'Memento Mori', the final
> couplet of the first version being,
>> Out of the deep resounds the hollow cry,
>> *Remember—oh, remember you must die!*
> . . . and there were many other revisions and versions (p.217).

Alec Warner, amateur sociologist, is concerned only to record
events with accuracy—having had his message repeated, he
'replaced the receiver a fraction before the other had done so'
(p.152). Charmian Piper, long accustomed to attention and
publicity, calmly assumes that her politely spoken prompting
has journalistic origins. (The press itself is meanwhile respond-
ing with more characteristic distortion and sensation-monger-
ing: 'The voice invariably warns the victim "You will die
to-night" ' (p.151).) And, most important of all, there are the
accepters, those such as Mortimer who says:

If I had my life over again I should form the habit of nightly composing myself to thoughts of death. I would practise, as it were, the remembrance of death. There is no other practice which so intensifies life. Death, when it approaches, ought not to take one by surprise. It should be part of the full expectancy of life. Without an ever-present sense of death life is insipid (p.166);

and Jean Taylor, safe from the calls in hospital but finding a personal memento mori in 'the senile group' (p.188) of geriatrics at the far end of her ward, who observes: 'It's difficult for people of advanced years to start remembering they must die. It is best to form the habit while young' (p.36). Her Catholicism here chimes with the retired policeman's apparently agnostic stoicism. And these are the two attitudes the book endorses: the religious view, seeing death as an end in which there is a crucial beginning, 'the first of the four last things to be ever remembered' (p.246); and a more pagan interpretation, in which it is again redeemed from terrifying absurdity by seeming to belong to some necessary cycle. Emphasizing the progression of the generations, a harmony in which they placidly participate, the old making way for the young that they have helped to rear, the Mortimers, in marked contrast to all other characters, are seen, happy, with a grandchild. For them, age and death are simply parts of an inevitable natural process: just as, for Jean Taylor, they are parts of an inevitable supernatural one. And so, like her, they are free from the anxieties that dog so many people in this book, liberated, as accepters of mortality, to healthier life.

As is stressed by one of its three epigraphs, a quotation from the Penny Catechism:

Q. What are the four last things to be ever remembered?
A. The four last things to be ever remembered are Death, Judgment, Hell and Heaven,

Memento Mori is a novel much insistent on the need to come to terms with death, to live with it in mind, so learning true perspective and humility. But the work has other aspects, too, and other epigraphs which point the way to them: Yeats's frustrated cry at 'this caricature, Decrepit age' and an ironically employed piece of pious genuflection to the elderly from Traherne—'O what Venerable and Reverend Creatures did the Aged seem! Immortal Cherubims!'. In *Memento Mori*, as in all Mrs Spark's novels, metaphysical concerns coexist with shrewd and very funny social observation. Its didactic diagrams are generously filled out. Age, here, and death are not abstractions: they appear clothed in wizened, documentary detail. The technique of character-portrayal is, for instance, very pertinent, most of the novel's septuagenarian personnel shown as now apparently consumed by one dominating quality: Jean Taylor's moral intelligence, Godfrey Colston's selfishness, Lettie's domineering will, Charmian's kindness, Mannering's devotion to his art, Warner's scientific curiosity. Time, it seems, has shrivelled down softer characteristics until only the spine of personality remains, standing out stark and unmistakable. And this gives opportunities for satire that are quickly taken up. The book is full of monitory vignettes of the doomed ego still insistently clamouring even in the shadow of the grave: Tempest Sidebottome, imperious on committees, as the cancer grows inside her; Mrs Pettigrew, after her first stroke, pushing for priority in meal-queues. The deep, resistant roots of self-concern are constantly exposed. The tenacity of vanity is spotlit, sometimes harshly: 'Lisa Brooke died in her seventy-third year after her second stroke. She had taken nine months to die, and in fact it was only a year before her death that, feeling rather ill, she had decided to reform her life, and reminding herself how attractive she still was, offered up the new idea, her celibacy to the Lord to whom no gift whatsoever is unacceptable' (p.15); at other times, more gently: 'Granny Green would never fail to tell the nurses after her hair was done. "I had a lovely head of hair till you cut it off," although in reality there had been very little to cut off' (p.122). Husks of appetite litter the narrative: domination-urges guttering out in feebly brandished will-forms; lust dwindled to the contemplation of a glittering suspender-tip. And, alongside the sharp-cut cameos of moral debility, stand pictures of physical decline and weakness. The arduous bodily struggles of the aged—'How primitive . . . life becomes in old age, when one may be surrounded by familiar comforts and yet more vulnerable to the action of nature than any young explorer at the Pole' (p.202)—are vividly recorded. Fittingly enough, disease and medical concerns pervade the book: it is dedicated to a nurse, and doctors and professional or amateur attendants are almost the only middle-aged or younger people in it. The mortality rate is high, six characters dying during the course of the novel and nearly all—there can rarely have been a less open-ended fiction—finally and clinically accounted for:

What were they sick, what did they die of?
Lettie Coston . . . comminuted fractures of the skull; Godfrey Colston, hypostatic pneumonia, Charmian Colston, uraemia; Jean Taylor, myocardial degeneration; Tempest Sidebottome, carcinoma of the cervix; Ronald Sidebottome, carcinoma of the bronchus; Guy Leet, arteriosclerosis, Henry Mortimer, coronary thrombosis. . . .' (p.246).

But, though the work does show the difficulties, the humiliations and dependencies that lay in wait for these reluctant transients as life draws towards its close, it is not limited to the depressing attributes of age. The vices of the vicious may, like arteries, harden with time's passing, but pleasant qualities also survive. Jean Taylor's 'continuing intelligence amongst the ruins' (p.68), Charmian's charity, Guy Leet's verve, things such as these much relieve the darkness of the picture. And, though dissolution steadily gains ground, there are those who respond with courage and with dignity to their afflictions and their helplessness. The scene in which Charmian, 'blissfully alone' (p.142) for once, painfully and slowly goes about the business of preparing tea, resting after every slight exertion then determinedly continuing, registers, with effective quietness, one such small but far from negligible triumph of human persistence.

Memento Mori makes a fairly comprehensive catalogue of age's features and effects, but, as the part played by Alec Warner indicates, there is more to the novel than this. Throughout the book, he is shown to parallel the author in another discipline. After all, he, too, is studying old age, making notes and keeping detailed dossiers: 'Old Age', it is said, '. . . had been his study since he had turned seventy' (p.60). But there is an important distinction. We hear of 'Alec's awe and curiosity being directed exclusively towards the human specimen' (p.185), and it is remarked how 'scientific observation differed from humane observation, and how the same people observed in these respective senses, actually seemed to be different people' (p.239). Warner's rigid insistence on physiological fact, it soon becomes apparent, entails a great deal of blindness to normal human response. He leaves out too much. His records, because of what they fail to include, are as off-key, as faintly absurd, as his behaviour sometimes is: and so, ironically pointing to the use-lessness of these 'factual' notes, these incomplete and un-arranged statistics, Mrs Spark finally throws them to the flames, lets them be reduced to ash by a fire that breaks out in Alec's flat.

The author's own study of old age is something very different. Including Warner's documentary details, it also goes beyond them. Taking account of areas he quite ignores, it is more sympathetic, treats its case-histories with greater warmth. And, of course, it is artistic, both in its concentration on a small society of characters woven wittily and pleasingly together, and in its elegant and mannered tone. Jean Taylor, we are told at one point, 'mused upon her condition and upon old age in general. Why do some people lose their memories, some their hearing? Why do some talk of their youth and others of their wills?' (pp.9–10). And the whole novel is, in effect, a medita-tion of this kind, a meditation in both general and more local terms. The large facts of age and death—the troubling abstrac-tions—are pondered; and, at the same time, incidentals and particulars—how certain types of personality under certain social conditions respond to their approaching end—are conveyed to the reader. The line around the subject is quite firmly drawn; the first chapter ends with the exchange:

> 'Oh, Taylor, how old are you?' said Charmian.
> 'Sixty-nine, Mrs. Colston,' said Mrs. Anthony.
> 'When will you be seventy?'
> 'Twenty-eighth November.'
> 'That will be splendid, Taylor. You will then be one of us,' said Charmian' (p.7).

For the most part, the under-seventies are only allowed to figure in the novel in so far as they display relevant reactions to old age. They are, like Sister Burstead, nervously middle-aged, apprehensively regarding the grim terrain ahead. Or they are parasitic: the book presents quite a gamut of exploit-ers, from benignly mercenary Olive through to more distasteful vampires such as Gwen or Eric and culminating in the burglars who rob and murder Lettie.

Full of period reference—to Nineties poets, Gaiety Girls, royalty at Cannes—this is a novel with long avenues back into the past, the flash-backs standard in Mrs Spark's fiction here covering greater expanses than usual even for her. The minds of these old characters convincingly stray back to long-gone quarrels, triumphs, love-affairs: Miss Valvona is not alone in that her 'eyes stared through her spectacles into the past'(p.39). The dead, especially the monstrous Lisa Brooke, so vital in the minds of their contemporaries, still seem to linger on. And, fittingly, it is wills, those last attempts to keep a grip on life and on the living, that give the plot recurrent impetus, pull it into more and more elaborate entanglement. Fondness for the appropriate extends, too, to the way in which some of these characters shuffle off their mortal coil, several, as by poetic justice, meeting with what Barbara Vaughan in *The Mandelbaum Gate* thinks of as 'an indigenous sort of death'.[5] Lettie Colston, for instance, brutal and domineering in her life, is brutally dispatched; the sadism in her excited demands for a return to harsher punishments horribly materializes round her; her lurid fantasies, steeped in thoughts of violence and malevolent conspiracy, finally attract lurid reality—burglars break into her bedroom, and: 'The man by the dressing-table hesitated nervily for a moment, then swiftly he was by Lettie's side. She opened wide her mouth and her yellow and brown eyes. He wrenched the stick from the old woman's hand and, with the blunt end of it, battered her to death. It was her eighty-first year' (pp.199–200). Godfrey, too, stubbornly selfish through his life, achieves a selfish death: 'Godfrey died . . . as the result of a motor accident, his car having collided with another at a bend in Kensington Church Street. He was not killed outright, but died a few days later of pneumonia which had set in from the shock. It was the couple in the other car who were killed outright' (p.245). And there are happier ends that are still apt—that of Henry Mortimer, for instance. A liking for natural physical activity, gardening, fishing, yachting, having been emphasized, he finally dies going aboard the boat that has given him so much enjoyment.

Always, the book's effects are beautifully controlled, as, for example, when geriatrics are introduced into the Maud Long

Ward, a scene where the novel suddenly shifts its perspective. Earlier, the subjects of the book have been presented as extremely aged, victims of the worst that time can inflict. Then, neatly, as the cots roll in, everything is put into new alignment; we are reminded that there can be further steps before the grave is reached:

> while the preparations were still in progress, this end of the ward was referred to among the nurses as the 'geriatric corner'.
> 'What's that word mean they keep saying?' Granny Roberts demanded of Miss Taylor.
> 'It's to do with old age. There must be some very old patients coming in.'
> 'We supposed to be teenagers, then?'
> Granny Valvona said, 'Our new friends will probably be centenarians' (pp.126–7).

At the hoary heart of this old world is the spectacle of utter senility: sardonically exorcising Traherne's cherubims, the pathetic scene in which Mrs Bean celebrates her hundredth birthday:

> 'Yes,' Granny Bean answered them in her far-away flute, 'I've lived a long time.'
> 'Yes,' said Granny Bean, 'I'm very happy.'
> 'That's right,' she agreed, 'I seen Queen Victoria once as a girl.'
> 'What does it feel like to be a hundred, Mrs. Bean?'
> 'All right,' she said weakly, nodding her head (p.242).

With this kind of inconsequence on the horizon, the prospect for those who have no religious faith to sustain them, no family to spend their final days with, is bleak indeed.

Yoked to increasing debility, the isolation so common in the books of Mrs Spark is shown to give rise to a situation of some grimness. Few of the characters here have anyone to turn to for support or consolation. Alec Warner, Jean Taylor, Lettie Colston are unmarried; Percy Mannering is apparently a widower; Guy Leet's marriage was unconsummated travesty. Apart from the Mortimers, the only surviving union we see, that of Charmian and Godfrey, is completely hollow, its links merely habit on the one side and resentment on the other. As the faculties Godfrey is so obsessed by gradually deteriorate, these people become ripe prey for exploitation: especially as blackmail once again threads through the narrative, trapping those who, unlike Charmian, a typical Spark protagonist, 'had not taken care, long before . . . old age, to destroy all possibly embarrassing documents' (p.137).

For all this, though, the book is finally exhilarating, no mere black record of humanity ground down by age, disintegrating into death. The fact that this material, so difficult to contemplate, has been brought under the control of intellect, worked into art—sifted, scrutinized, given pleasing order—represents achievement of some mental fortitude. Behind the flicker of its comedy, the clear-eyed witty stoicism of *Memento Mori* demonstrates a dignified and brave response to time's inevitable gangrene. Certainly, the writing of the novel seems to have entailed some strain for, Mrs Spark has said, in the book that followed it, she deliberately turned to something she considered less demanding: 'Next, I wanted to give my mind a holiday and to write something light and lyrical—as near a poem as a novel could get, and in as few words as possible.'[6]

The result was *The Ballad of Peckham Rye*, a work in which the catalyst changes from death on the telephone to a devil in south London. Dougal Douglas, the central figure of this novel, is invested with traditional diabolic attributes. On his head are two small lumps—relics, he claims, of horns that have been surgically removed—and one of his shoulders is deformed, higher than the other. 'It's my belief,' a character affirms, 'that Dougal Douglas is a diabolic agent, if not in fact the Devil' (p.112)[7]: and the subject of the charge obligingly does everything to aid this impression—strolling through a cemetery, for instance, he makes a point of posing on a tombstone 'like an angel-devil, with his hump shoulder and gleaming smile, and his fingers of each hand widespread against the sky (p.36); talking to a fellow-boarder, he 'gazed at him like a succubus whose mouth is its eyes' (p.32); and he even openly declares himself to be 'one of the wicked spirits that wander through the world for the ruin of souls' (p.106).

He is aided in this mission by three jobs he undertakes during his stay in Peckham: ghost writer, human-researcher, and investigator into the industrial environment. The first of these is financed by Maria Cheeseman, a retired actress. Fabricating her life-story by careful distortion of incidents from his own and others' experience, Dougal occasionally encounters opposition, not so much on the grounds that what he produces is false (Miss Cheeseman is in fact rather eager for her real age to be camouflaged and her early years in a Streatham shoe factory to be omitted) as that it is unflattering or embarrassing. 'If you only want to write a straight autobiography,' he responds, 'you should have got a straight ghost. I'm crooked' (p.104), but eventually he does turn up the cliché-coated piece of cosiness desired, having first, to help him towards this, compiled a small anthology of 'Phrases suitable for Cheese' (p.126), candied idioms of the 'I was too young at the time to know why my mother was crying' order. This gives opportunity for parody: 'I felt a grim satisfaction as the cab which bore me and my few poor belongings bowled across Vauxhall Bridge and into the great world—capital G capital W—ahead full stop. Yes comma Peckham had been fun exclamation mark' (pp.180–1). It is important, too, since the way in which people are given to muffling truth with inauthentic words, editing reality for their own consolation, is the novel's major theme. Miss Cheese-man is unusual only in that she can afford to pay someone to tint her life with ego-gratifying misrepresentation. Others have to do it for themselves—Mavis Crewe, for instance:

> 'You could have knocked me over,' she said. 'I was just giving Dixie her tea; it was, I should say, twenty past five and there was a ring at the bell. I said to Dixie, "Whoever can that be?" So I went to the door, and lo and behold there he was on the doorstep. He said, "Hallo, Mavis," he said. I said, "You just hop it, you." He said, "Can I see Dixie?" I said, "You certainly can't," I said. I said, "You're a dirty swine. You remove yourself." I said, "and don't show your face again," I said. He said, "Come on, Mavis." I said, "Mrs. Crewe to you," and I shut the door in his face' (pp.7–8);

or Mavis's daughter, Dixie (p.42), or Merle Coverdale herself, routed ogress of Dixie's narratives, quick-tongued star per-former in her own (pp.135–6).

Reality in this novel, as in these monologues (compare the actual events—page 1—with Mavis's account of them) is frequently shown to be buried below deep strata of accumulated falsity. Before truth can be reached, accretions must be cleared, some excavation must take place, rather like that going on in Nun Lane throughout the book, mentioned now and then; yielding, we are told, 'interesting finds and human remains' (p.182); and reaching completion, with some neatness, just as Dougal moves away from Peckham, his own bringing-to-light accomplished too. Words, phrases, idioms: these continually refract the truth. Dougal, presented as a man alert to verbal fraud—'You've changed,' he says to Jinny, his ex-girlfriend. 'You are using words like "sweet" and "thrilled"' (p.170)—enters a community where speech has largely blurred into jargon: Humphrey's text-book technicalities—'You aren't likely to have a dispute at Meadows, Meade and Grindley. You might have an issue, though' (p.30); Druce's prim-mouthed euphemisms—'you'll be in touch with the workers, or rather, as we prefer to say, our staff' (p.16); Joyce Willis's candour-floss—'Quite frankly, the first time Richard invited you to dinner I knew we'd found the answer. Richard didn't see it at first, quite frankly, but I think he's beginning to see it now' (p.165); and of course those words that fleck the dialogue like leit motifs, 'ignorant' and 'immoral'. 'Have you observed, Mr. Willis,' asks Dougal, 'the frequency with which your employees use the word "immoral"? Have you noticed how equally often they use the word "ignorant"? These words are significant . . . psychologically and sociologically' (p.116). And what is significant about them is that, camouflaging generalities, these vague, complacent adjectives—catchwords of a torpid tribe—are symptoms of real ignorance, true immorality.

Into a society of cliché and hypocrisy, self-deceit and tightly blinkered prejudice, Dougal is dispatched, paid by two textile concerns 'to bring vision into the lives of the workers' (p.15), 'to take the pulse of the people and plumb the industrial depths of Peckham' (p.16), 'to discover the spiritual well-spring, the glorious history of the place' (p.17). The way in which he conducts this 'human research' (p.18), tries to provoke 'an enlargement of the total perceptive capacity' (p.99), is by a series of didactic theatricals. 'Actions,' he observes in a notebook, are 'more effective than words. Enact everything. Depict' (p.128). To characters engaged in warding off reality with hand-me-down vocabulary and self-consoling misrepresentation, he offers graphic display of facts only reluctantly acknowledged:

renders disquietingly vivid experiences they prefer to keep in mental mist. His mimes and histrionic skills call loud attention to truths pushed into cloudy corners of the mind: and many cannot face this. Tears fall copiously as Dougal circulates; fights occur; a wedding comes to grief; paranoia seethes up to explosion; there are breakdowns; savage death is caused. Suppressed violence, suspicions, jailed emotions, all are conjured out into the open: for, through his plottings and his pantomimes, Dougal acts as exorcist, as he himself points out:

> 'I have powers of exorcism,' Dougal said. . . . 'The ability to drive devils out of people.'
> 'I thought you were a devil yourself.'
> 'The two states are not incompatible,' (p.142).

Of those in his orbit only Elaine Kent—and she is, the novel several times reminds us, 'an experienced controller of process' (pp.52, 55, 84)—remains impervious to his nerve-assaults:

> 'There's a gang watching out for you,' Elaine said. 'So be careful where you go at nights. I shouldn't go out alone much.'
> 'Terrifying, isn't it? I mean, say this is the street and there's Trevor over there. And say here's Collie Gould crossing the road, and young Leslie comes up to me and asks the time and I look at my watch. Then out jumps Trevor with a razor—rip, rip, rip. But Collie whistles loud on his three fingers. Leslie gives me a parting kick where I lie in the gutter and slinks after Trevor away into the black concealing night. Up comes the copper and finds me. The cop takes one look, turns away, and pukes on the pavement. He then with trembling fingers places a whistle to his lips.'
> 'Sit down and stop pushing the good furniture about', she said (p.184).

With her calm and commonsense, Elaine is very different from the book's eventual casualties, those who fall prey to Dougal's machinations. 'What guilty wee consciences you've all got' (p.179), he at one point says of these: and, having noted this, sets out to find the cause of their unrest, seeks the Achilles heel, the 'fatal flaw' (p.26), the weak spot in personalities otherwise quite firmly armoured in conventional behaviour and response: Miss Frierne's guilt about her long-lost brother, Druce's furtive sexual perversity, Merle's loneliness and fear of her employer-lover. When Dougal strikes at these vulnerabilities, he meets with no resistance.

And this debility, it is suggested, is an unavoidable result of the society in which these people live. 'Peckham', Dougal observes, 'must have a moral character of its own' (p.94). The novel shows it is a stultifying one. The community, set out in some detail and complexity, is stagnant and afflicted by an epidemic lack of honesty. Perception of the world around, of the environment, is almost minimal, something stressed quite early in the book when Dougal takes Merle Coverdale, long an inhabitant of Peckham, walking round the district:

> Dougal pointed to a house on the right. 'There's a baby's pram,' he said, 'stuck out on a balcony which hasn't any railings.'
> She looked and sure enough there was a pram perched on an open ledge only big enough to hold it, outside a second-floor window. She said, 'They ought to be prosecuted. There's a baby in that pram, too.'
> 'No, it's only a doll,' Dougal said.
> 'How do you know?'
> 'I've seen it before. The house is a baby-carriage works. The pram is only for show.'
> 'Oh, it gave me a fright.'
> 'How long have you lived in Peckham?' he said.
> 'Twelve and a half years.'
> 'You've never noticed the pram before?'
> 'No, can't say I have. Must be new.'
> 'From the style of the pram, it can't be new. In fact the pram has been there for twenty-five years. You see, you simply haven't noticed it' (p.39).

Lack of awareness, somnambulistic drifting of this kind, is typical. The whole area seems drained of its vitality. Juxtaposed with glints from a colourful past—Miss Frierne's anecdotes about her youth, Dougal's references to local history: 'Mendelssohn wrote his "Spring Song" in Ruskin Park. Mrs. Fitzherbert lived in Camberwell Grove. Boadicea committed suicide on Peckham Rye probably where the bowling green is now, I should imagine' (p.32)—the present appears sadly lacklustre, as emerges most clearly in the midsummer night chapter, where routine manoeuvrings of contemporary lust are damagingly pushed into perspective by the date when they occur. Prefacing each with a reminder of the festal day, the narrative pauses on three scenes of dulled encounter:

Miss Merle Coverdale opened the door of her flat on Denmark Hill, and admitted Mr. Druce in the early evening of midsummer's day. . . . Merle switched on the television and found a play far advanced. They watched the fragment of the play as they drank their coffee. Then they went into the bedroom and took off their clothes in a steady rhythm. Merle took off her cardigan and Mr. Druce took off his coat. Merle went to the wardrobe and brought out a green quilted silk dressing-gown. Mr. Druce went to the wardrobe and found his blue dressing-gown with white spots. Merle took off her blouse and Mr. Druce his waistcoat. Merle put the dressing-gown over her shoulders and, concealed by it, took off the rest of her clothes, with modest gestures. Mr. Druce slid his braces and emerged from his trousers. These he folded carefully and, padding across the room to the window, laid them on a chair. He made another trip bearing his waistcoat and jacket which he placed over the back of the chair.

They stayed in bed for an hour, in the course of which Merle twice screamed because Mr. Druce had once pinched and once bit her. 'I'm covered with marks as it is,' she said (pp.69–70);

after which:

A western breeze blew over the Rye and it was midsummer night, a Saturday. Humphrey carried the two tartan rugs from his car while Dixie walked by his side, looking to left and right and sometimes turning to see if the path was clear of policemen. . . . Humphrey spread a rug and she sat down upon it. She lifted the fringe and started to pull at it, separating the matted threads. . . . Humphrey pulled her towards him, and started to unbutton her coat. She buttoned it up again. 'I'm cold,' she said.

'Oh, come on, Dixie,' he said.

'Connie Weedin got an increment,' she said. 'I've got to wait for my increment till August. I only found out through the girl that does the copy die-stamp operation and had the staff salaries' balance sheet to do' (pp.71–2);

and also:

On midsummer night Trevor Lomas walked with a somnambulistic sway into Findlater's Ballroom and looked round for Beauty. The floor was expertly laid and polished. The walls were pale rose, with concealed lighting. Beauty stood on the girls' side, talking to a group of very similar and lustrous girls. They had prepared themselves for this occasion with diligence, and as they spoke together, they did not smile much nor attend to each other's words. As an accepted thing, any of the girls might break off in the middle of a sentence, should a young man approach her, and, turning to him, might give him her entire and smiling regard' (pp.75–6).

Life nourished by such things—stale habit, money-greed— will be anaemic and unable to stand strain. Seeking the disease which visibly spreads its enervation everywhere around him, Dougal finally claims that 'the moral element lay at the root of all industrial discontents' (p.114), and then, elaborating this, goes on to sketch a framework of behaviour-codes prevailing in this area, skeletons the novelist has already and sardonically fleshed out:

There are four types of morality observable in Peckham. . . . One, emotional. Two, functional. Three, puritanical. Four, Christian. . . . Take the first category, Emotional. Here, for example, it is considered immoral for a man to live with a wife who no longer appeals to him. Take the second, Functional, in which the principal factor is class solidarity such as, in some periods and places, has also existed amongst the aristocracy, and of which the main manifestation these days is the trade union movement. Three, Puritanical, of which there are several modern variants, monetary advancement being the most prevalent gauge of the moral life in this category. Four, Traditional, which accounts for about one per cent of the Peckham population and which in its simplest form is Christian. All moral categories are of course intermingled. Sometimes all are to be found in the beliefs and behaviour of one individual (pp.114–5).

With only parody moralities of this kind to fall back on—in a society dominated by heavy conformity-pressures and that getting-on ethic of which Dixie, with her savings and aspirations to a model bungalow, is such a savagely observed disciple—people have nothing genuine to help them cope with awkward aspects of their personality, no alternative but to suppress. They take refuge from reality in verbal camouflage or spurious social roles: and, if stripped of this defensive hypocrisy, react first with self-pity, then with either violence or breakdown.

Dougal's function in the book is to apply the goad, create moments of truth by engineering situations in which characters are forced to experience sharp facts of life. And briefly he succeeds. The torpid are galvanized into sincerity. Humphrey sees Dixie as she is; Miss Frierne, Druce, and Merle experience the hurt of honesty. But the lesson is a temporary one. When Dougal is gone, life in Peckham swiftly lapses back into coma. Deceits begin again; inauthenticity returns. Humphrey, having refused his bride at the altar-rails, re-appears and marries her; Dixie, detester of the living Merle, begins, after the woman's death, unctuously to refer to 'Poor Miss Coverdale' (p.199). Events dim into myth: 'in any case, within a few weeks, everyone forgot the details' (p.12) and:

> Some said Humphrey came back and married the girl in the end. Some said, no, he married another girl. Others said, it was like this, Dixie died of a broken heart and he never looked at another girl again. Some thought he had returned, and she had slammed the door in his face and called him a dirty swine, which he was. One or two recalled there had been a fight between Humphrey and Trevor Lomas. But at all events everyone remembered how a man had answered 'No' at his wedding (pp.201-2).

'The affair', we are told, 'is a legend referred to from time to time in the pubs' (p.12). What has happened becomes a story, fiction, a ballad.

Of course, as Mrs Spark is very much aware, it is not just the characters portrayed who pull events into a shape that gives them satisfaction. She herself is also doing this, as the title of her novel intimates and its procedures underline—the emphasis on dialogue and marked reliance on the 'he said—she said' formula:

'Get away from here, you dirty swine,' she said.

'There's a dirty swine in every man,' he said.

'Showing your face round here again,' she said.

'Now, Mavis, now, Mavis,' he said.

She was seen to slam the door in his face, and he to press the bell, and she to open the door again (p.1).

Here we are deliberately reminded of the novel's nearness to the ballad, word-of-mouth literature, retailing of events to some immediate audience: that oral culture which survives, debased to gossip, embedded with blunted kennings, in the industrial community of Peckham. But there are also more sophisticated techniques in evidence. Carefully marshalled, omens, ironies, forewarnings whisper through the book, and cluster thickly round doomed Merle, who is taken for walks through cemeteries, left waiting in a 'hall which was lined with wood like a coffin' (p.177), has sharp objects meditatively trained in her direction by her later killer, and, just before the murder, unconsciously approaching classic metaphor, remarks, 'I'll have a glass of red wine. I feel I need something red to buck me up' (p.190). Dougal, too, is shown insistently as acting like a novelist: not just in the fictional career he is constructing for Miss Cheeseman, but also in the basic contrivance of his 'human research': his liking for plots, for pushing people into situations where, pressured, their true nature must emerge. In later life, we are even mockingly assured, he became a writer—one working to that thrifty pattern Mrs Spark so much approves: 'for economy's sake, he gathered together the scrap ends of his profligate experience—for he was a frugal man at heart—and turned them into a lot of cock-eyed books' (p.201). And, while in Peckham, he tells lies, schemes, and manipulates just as the novelist herself does, the activities of both being obliquely denounced by Nelly Mahone, the book's vagrant Irish revivalist: ' "Six things," Nelly declaimed, "there are which the Lord detesteth. Haughty eyes, a lying tongue, hands that shed innocent blood. . . . A heart that deviseth wicked plots, feet that are swift to run into mischief. . . . A deceitful witness that uttereth lies. . . . And him that soweth discord among brethren" ' (p.150). These, as Mrs Spark well knows, are the stock-in-trade of writers of her kind: but they have, she feels too, their justification. The haughty judging eyes, the lies and plots, the invented complications and slaughterings of the imaginary are all subordinate to a didactic purpose, for, as Nelly also proclaims: 'The words of the double-tongued are as if they were harmless, but they reach even to the inner part of the bowels' (p.187). Parables, products of the double-tongued, teach as well as entertain: and, if this end is properly achieved, the superficially false means are vindicated. A fiction about the way that people hate cold fact and try to stave it off with fictions of their own, *The Ballad of Peckham Rye* parades its unreal nature, fits, like a pot its mould, Mrs Spark's description of her work: 'I keep in my mind specifically that what I am writing is fiction because I am interested in truth—absolute truth—and I don't pretend that what I am writing is more than an imaginative extension of the truth—something inventive.'[8] Far more than *The Comforters*, of which the author has said, 'I wrote a novel to work out the technique first, to sort of make it all right with myself to write a novel at all—a novel about writing a novel',[9] it conforms to this description, proves itself as a fiction that through stressed lies, emphasized distortions, makes a plea for truth and honesty.

This is the framework of the parable, a structure overlaid by comic and satiric detailing of life in Peckham (an area bordering on Mrs Spark's home at the time she wrote the book). Moving easily from the very old world of *Memento Mori* to a predominantly young one, from the realm of crematoria, dated literary styles, and paid companions to a milieu of jive, razors, and drape jackets, the novelist maps the social, physical and moral geography of Peckham. At times, the tone is like that of some anthropologist's dispatch, alert notation of the tribal rituals: 'Dixie and Elaine stared at the girl as she slid out of her coat and let it fall on the back of the chair. They stared as if by duty, and watched every detail. The girl was aware of this, and seemed to expect it' (p.55). More usually, the accent is satiric, as, for instance, in the scene where the novel briefly shifts its searchlight from working-class *moeurs* to a specimen of middle-class vapidity. Joyce Willis, wife of one of Dougal's employers, has invited him to dinner, and, while they wait for the husband to arrive, Mrs Spark, sharply trapping each nuance of egotism and vacuity, sets the woman moving round the room in a little stir of vanity and snobbery, both audible: ' "One of Richard's great mistakes—I'm speaking to you quite frankly," she said, "was insisting on our *living* in Peckham. Well, the house is all right—but I mean, the environment. There are simply no people in the place. Our friends always get lost finding the way here; they drive round for hours. And there are blacks at the other end of the Avenue, you know. I mean, it's so silly" ' (p.166); and visible: 'She filled both glasses with sherry, turning the good bones of her wrists and holding the glasses at the end of her long fingers with their lacquered nails and the bright emerald. She looked at herself, before she sat down, in the gilt-framed glass and turned back a wisp of her short dark-gold hair. Her face was oval; she posed it to one side' (p.167). From this brocaded interior to the squalor of Nelly Mahone's room in Lightbody Buildings, the novel charts a network of community, demonstrates the 'classes within classes in Peckham' (p.33), where these overlap, and what happens when they do: 'Dixie sat with Humphrey, Dougal and Elaine Kent in Costa's Café. . . . "I've felt tired all day," she said. She addressed the men, ignoring Elaine as she had done all evening, because Elaine was factory' (pp.54–5). The industrial environment of Peckham, which the novel shows to be so enervating, is depicted with both relish and thoroughness. But, as the title reminds, there is more to the place than urban sprawl. Peckham is best known for its Rye: and a local landmark, lavish grassland, of this kind is something that, for Mrs Spark, cannot be ignored. Of her native Edinburgh, in a passage showing well her tendency to treat the world as metaphor, she once wrote:

> But the physical features of the place surely had an effect as special as themselves on the outlook of the people. The Castle Rock is something, rising up as it does from pre-history between the formal grace of the New Town and the noble network of the Old. To have a great primitive black crag rising up in the middle of populated streets of commerce, stately squares and winding closes, is like the statement of an unmitigated fact preceded by 'nevertheless'.[10]

In a similar way, lying at the heart of the factories and houses, 'the dusky scope of the Rye's broad lyrical acres' (p.5) can speak to the perceptive. Providing, through the book, a casual background to strolls and brawls and would-be love-making on tartan rugs, it glows, as the novel ends, into a greater consequence: 'it was a sunny day for November, and, as he drove swiftly past the Rye, he saw the children playing there and the women coming home from work with their shopping-bags, the Rye for an instant looking like a cloud of green and gold, the people seeming to ride upon it, as you might say there was another world than this' (p.202). The commonplace, so assiduously and wittily depicted, is transfigured; we are reminded that these things are parable; the essential latent in accidentals is allowed its brief epiphany. And in her next book *The Bachelors*, a novel which appeared the same year, it is to this union of the natural and the supernatural, the way in which they are, for her, inextricably linked, that Mrs Spark very much turns her attention.

To a considerable extent, *The Bachelors* would seem to owe its genesis to a passage from her article on Proust:

> It could be abundantly demonstrated that present-day Christian creative writing, that which is most involved in an attempt to combat materialism, reflects a materialism of its own; this takes the form of a dualistic attitude towards matter and spirit. They are seen too much in moral conflict, where the spirit triumphs by virtue of disembodiment. This is really an amoral conception of spirit.[11]

It is also, in its discarding of the tangible and visible as waste, a most uneconomic view of life, and so one much opposed to Mrs Spark's philosophy: that voiced for her in *The Bachelors* by Matthew Finch, a Jesuit-educated Catholic who claims, 'You've got to affirm the oneness of reality in some form or another' (p.89).[12] The book in which he figures, though, is thronged with instances of this imperative being ignored. Narrowing in on that invidious apartheid so deplored in her Proust essay, Mrs Spark puts at the centre of her work a creed in which this segregation of the earthly from the supernatural can be very clearly seen. Her novel deals with spiritualism, a faith which, as its name suggests and its devotees continually proclaim, is utterly opposed to the material. Throughout the book, in varying tones, attention is drawn to this. Freda Flower, for instance, the widow whose trepidant doubts about the fate of her savings have attracted legal scrutiny towards the Sanctuary of Light, is asked reprovingly, 'musn't we subordinate our materialistic endeavours to those of the spirit?'

(p.25), and warned in séance, 'Let the sister beware of false friends and materialistic advice. The letter killeth but the spirit giveth life' (p.36). Across the mind of Matthew Finch, havering on the guilty verge of sex, farcically glides the thought that 'A spiritualist girl might dematerialise in the act' (p.55). And, more sombrely, we learn that Seton, the medium, shocked earlier to find his mother 'a materialist at heart' (p.172), is now dangerously exasperated when his girl-friend, Alice, talks about marriage 'as if he were a materialist with a belief in empty forms' (p.174).

Constantly fencing off the natural from the supernatural, spiritualism is for Mrs Spark just as misguided as—in fact, merely a subtler instance of—that materialism her séance-frequenters haughtily dismiss. Her ideal is more thrifty, a philosophy which combats dualism and, as it were, salvages the everyday by seeing it as permeated by the spiritual. 'I haven't a strong sense of distinction between natural and supernatural;' she has said. 'I think we're all involved in the supernatural world'[13]: and her Catholicism reinforces this. 'There are only two religions, the spiritualist and the Catholic,' announces Ronald Bridges, the writer's persona in this novel, adding 'You must take it in a figurative sense' (p.190). And what he means is that a religious creed either affirms 'the oneness of reality', as with Catholicism—'One of the things which interested me particularly about the Church', Mrs Spark has written, 'was its acceptance of matter. So much of our world rejects it'[14]—or, as with spiritualism, separates, like chaff from wheat, the mundane from the other-worldly. Repeatedly, the novel's spiritualists are shown vaunting their detachment from the world. Socket, the counterfeit clergyman plainly declares, 'I have no wish to impede the course of the laws of the kingdom, but the laws of the spirit come first' (p.136): and the implications of this antinomian code, with its emphasis on motive not fact, uncoil around Seton and his plan to murder Alice. In his early years, we are told, Patrick, a spiritual youth, found himself revolted by reality:

> Mary Rose by J. M. Barrie is Patrick's favourite, and he is taken to the theatre to see it acted and is sharply shocked by the sight of the real actresses and actors with painted faces performing outwardly on the open platform this tender

romance about the girl who was stolen by the fairies on a Hebridean island. As a young man he memorises the early poems of W. B. Yeats and will never forget them. Now, on his first enchanted visit to the Western Isles he first encounters an unfortunate occurrence, having sat up reciting to an American lady far into the night and the next morning being accused of having taken money from her purse. He is thinking of her, in his poetic innocence, as a kindred soul to whom money does not matter, but now she carries on as if money mattered. . . . Another little while, and he has sex relations with a woman, and is upset by all the disgusting details and is eventually carried away into transports. There is a lot of nasty stuff in life which comes breaking up our ecstasy, our inheritance (pp.171–2).

Accordingly, as medium, he devotes himself to hiving off the spirit from the squalidly material. And when the time arrives at which it would be easier if Alice were destroyed, he is able to see his scheme as an extension of this: not murder, but a process of benign disintegration, disentangling of the soul from all the body's dross. 'I will release her spirit from this gross body' (p.174), he tells himself complacently, letting his mind browse on images of the girl's death or 'the liberation of Alice's spirit' (p.210), as he translates it to himself, proud in the convenient belief that 'It was godlike to conquer the body, to return it to the earth' (p.238). Unaware of the extremes towards which Seton's creed is elbowing him, Matthew Finch, putting his religious schooling to good use, still manages to diagnose just what is going wrong: ' "He has no intention of marrying her at all," Matthew said, becoming fierily convinced of it. "What do you expect of a spiritualist? His mind's attuned to the ghouls of the air all day long. How can he be expected to consider the moral obligations of the flesh? The man's a dualist. No sacramental sense" ' (p.89).

It is in connection with this dualism, a keeping separate in preference to uniting, that the title and its implications fall into their place. 'I wrote a book about bachelors and it seemed to me that everyone was a bachelor,'[15] said Mrs Spark: and certainly, braiding its plot around a plexus of solitaries, her fiction here musters a generous assembly of the unattached. The paucity of partnerships usual in her writing is elaborated, with this book,

into a comprehensive dossier of celibates. There are ten unmarried men, 'bachelors of varying degrees of confirmation'
(p.16), or eleven, if the young priest standing in his porch uttering sociable inanities to the home-going faithful is included;
three single girls; two widows; and a divorcee. Together, they
compose an intricacy of alliances, intrigues and enmities, an
urban social web. But although they are pulled into some
community, basically they remain very much alone. This is
most chillingly conveyed, perhaps, by the tenth chapter of the
book in which Mrs Spark, employing a technique similar to
that used in her preceding work for the midsummer night
section, a brisk dealing out of damningly epitomizing scenes,
follows the progress of a city Sunday. This portrait of a day
begins, as the novel itself earlier opened, with a general overture
firmly establishing the metropolitan environment: 'Next day,
Sunday morning, Sunday afternoon and the long jaded evening—the very clocks seeming to yawn—occurred all over
London and especially in Kensington, Chelsea and Hampstead,
where there were newspapers, bells, talk, sleep, fate' (p.141).[16]
Then, weaving together all the work's major characters, a
tapestry depicting bachelors in company unrolls—Tim and
Hildegarde waking after a night together, she still talking of
Ronald; Ronald himself after church, reluctantly hearing out
Matthew's accounts of Elsie's sexual verve; Isobel and Martin
in the afternoon, bickering with Walter Prett; Ewart Thornton,
first dining with Marlene, then later in the evening garrulous
on the telephone to Freda; Socket and Garland arranging their
strategies; Patrick and Alice in her flat; and lastly, Ronald
confronting Elsie, an episode which ends as the day does: 'He
went down the stairs and out into the dark streets of Monday
morning' (p.186). Throughout this frieze, with the important
exception of the final section and despite the fact that each
scene is ostensibly one of friendship or of intimacy, runs a long
thread of betrayal. Hildegarde doesn't love Tim and will soon
leave him; Matthew, having already betrayed one of Ronald's
confidences to Elsie, now gossips irresponsibly about her;
Martin is swindling Isobel and she is lying to Walter; Ewart
will refuse to give evidence for either Marlene or Freda;
Socket is planning to abandon Garland; Patrick hopes to
murder Alice. Even, perhaps especially, when together these
people are isolated, vulnerable, and thrown back on themselves.

Stress, in Mrs Spark's portayal of this circle, falls heavily upon the sterile and the unproductive: upon homosexuality, contraception, and abortion, all of which are treated with distaste. The first, through Garland's painted posturings and Socket's seamy trading, emerges as sordid, furtive, or ridiculous. The second is denounced by Elsie: 'They fumble about with their french letters or they tear open their horrible little packets of contraceptives like kids with sweets, or they expect me to have a rubber stop-gap already fitted. All the time I want to be in love with the man and conceive his child, but I keep thinking of the birth-control and something inside me turns in its grave' (p.181). And the third, the most essential to the plot since Patrick is urging Alice to agree to an abortion, has, improperly performed, brought about the death of Gloria, Lyte's mistress in the past. 'There aren't any husbands that I know of,' (p.178) Elsie laments; the subjects of this book are 'fruitless souls' (p.240); and, once again, it is Matthew who offers the religious gloss:

'I'm afraid we are heretics,' he said, 'or possessed by devils.' His curls shone under the lamp. 'It shows a dualistic attitude, not to marry if you aren't going to be a priest or a religious. You've got to affirm the oneness of reality in some form or another.'

'We're not in fact heretics,' Ronald said, 'under the correct meaning of the term.'

'Well, we've got a heretical attitude, in a way' (p.89).

Marriage and Holy Orders, both unions, the Church being the Bride of Christ, are sacraments; celibacy is not.

Reasons for remaining single vary, of course, and *The Bachelors* therefore convenes quite a wide range of handicaps to happy and successful co-existence. Among these people, it is notable, behaviour-patterns frequently travesty the natural—for example, Ewart Thornton, the schoolmaster who gives dinner parties for prize pupils to placate maternal and house-wifely instincts fussing in his burly, tweeded frame, or turns to the telephone for gossipy, female companionship without commitment: 'His lips expanded in the chair, and his chin went into extra folds as his face sank into the skull. A smile of comfortable womanliness spread far into his cheeks as he spoke and his eyes were avid, as if they had never moved dispassionately over an examination paper. "Yes, Freda my dear, I made no bones about it and I just said to her, I said . . ." ' (p.162). Others remain fixed in roles of pre-maturity: Tim Raymond, a perpetual nephew; Martin Bowles, in middle age, still an over-mothered son. Barriers to intimacy are encountered everywhere. There can be fear of responsibility, for instance, as in Matthew Finch, or temperamental difficulties of the kind displayed by apoplectic Walter Prett. The ineffectualness of Francis Eccles with his mild and feckless drifting is one hindrance to satisfactory partnering: and sexual warping, from the blatancies of Garland or of Socket to Thornton's incongruous domesticities, is another. Egotism, represented at mentally sick extreme by Patrick Seton, can bar the way from singleness, and so can physical illness, as it does for Ronald Bridges.

The last is the case examined in most detail: and it is interesting because there are strong similarities implied between Ronald's situation and that of the novelist. He is, as the opening section of the book quickly establishes, an epileptic, kept somewhat apart from ordinary life and its ambitions by disease, but also given insight from the pain and tension this creates in him. Like a Romantic artist, Ronald sometimes regards himself as 'one possessed by a demon' (p.9); the convulsions that descend on him have notorious resemblance to the vatic frenzies of the oracle or sybil; he is a man who has been constantly pushed out of usual routine, normal involvement, and: 'In the course of time this experience sharpened his wits, and privately looking round at his world of acquaintances, he became, at certain tense moments, a truth-machine, under which his friends took on the aspect of demon-hypocrites' (p.9). And this use of the epileptic as a figure of the artist is strengthened by another element in the book: the resemblance between Ronald and Seton. In the early stages of the narrative points of contact between them are lightly pencilled in. Hildegarde, Ronald's girl-friend, patronizingly tells him, 'darling, you're a genius' (p.15): later, closing the equation, Marlene, patroness of Seton, assures him, 'you're a genius, Patrick' (p.30). The outward manifestations of epilepsy have similarities—upturned eyes, twitching limbs, frothing mouth—to the state of mediumistic trance. This likeness is first mentioned as if incidentally, merely a comic instance of the woman's monomania, when Ronald verges upon seizure in Marlene Cooper's flat—' "I do believe," she said, "that you are sensitive to the atmosphere of this flat. For a moment, just now, I thought you were going into a trance. I am psychic, you know. I'm certain you would make an excellent medium, if properly trained" ' (p.50)—and later driven home with fierce comedy in the trial scene. Throughout this, there has been insistence on the nature of a trance: 'you see, he's a medium. His eyes rolled upward and he foamed a bit at the mouth and his legs and arms twitched' (pp.214–5); and ' "Let us get this clear," said the judge. "A person in a state of trance as you call it, rolls up his or her eyes, foams at the mouth and twitches" ' (p.218). Then, beautifully placed and planned, Ronald, giving evidence, feels the oncoming of an epileptic turmoil:

He fumbled in his pockets for his pills. They were in his other suit at home. He gave up. He stumbled down the steps and fell two steps before he got to the bottom. There he foamed at the mouth. His eyes turned upward, and the drum-like kicking of his heels began on the polished wooden floor.

'Is this man a medium?' said the judge (p.221).

And the answer should be that in a sense he is: at least in those moments when his mind becomes a kind of geiger-counter registering with an urgency he cannot ignore—and much against his efforts to remain 'the amiable johnnie he had by then for the sake of sheer good will and protection from the world, affected to be' (p.9)—various degrees of human falsity.

As the book proceeds, the suggestion is elaborated that Ronald's disability, his wound, entails some compensatory penetration, has endowed him with more than ordinary perception: and that, in its turn, this gift can be uncomfortable, generating acrid states of mind such as that shown to torment him on returning from a party:

Ronald was suddenly obsessed by the party, and by the figures who had moved under Isobel's chandelier, and who, in Ronald's present mind, seemed to gesticulate like automatic animals; they made sociable noises which struck him as hysterical. Isobel's party stormed upon him like a play in which the actors have begun to jump off the stage, so that he was no longer simply the witness of a comfortable satire, but was suddenly surrounded by a company of ridiculous demons (p.116).

Just as Ronald's generally spectatorial attitude to life is rather like that of a writer, so his disgusted moments of heightened awareness mirror an artist's hypersensitivity. The terminology used of his predicament—his 'great melancholy boredom' (p.107), 'disgust, despair and brain-burning' (p.117), 'times of utter disenchantment' (p.121)—comes noticeably close to that applied in Mrs Spark's short story 'The Fathers' Daughters' to a sardonic novelist who has 'great depressions when he sat all day, staring and enduring, and all night miraculously wrote the ache out of his system in prose of harsh merriment'.[17] And his plight is, in fact, that of any social satirist. For such a writer, there must always be uneasy awareness that dilemmas solved in art—where exhilaration at accomplished ridicule attractively antidotes any despondency at the nature of what is being ridiculed—put up a more stubborn resistance out of it. Detachment, admirable in literature, is in life a more ambiguous achievement. The derisory and clearly labelled two-dimensionals of satire are also types of people who have to be lived with: and it is here the demanding problem starts: how to reconcile sharp awareness of human fallibility with charitable co-existence?

Ronald is not only a maimed perceptive. He is also, as an artist must accept that he is also, a man moving in society, subject to moral constraints, having responsibility to others. And, recording his behaviour in this sphere, Mrs Spark sets out clearly her ethical scheme. As a novelist, she has been frequently accused of misanthropy, malice aforethought towards her characters, a relish for detraction's sour delights. Through the behaviour of Ronald, whose personality and predicament are carefully brought close to those of a satiric writer, she both examines and refutes these charges. His moments of disgust are given in full violence but do not, it is stressed, drive him into cynicism or spring from any malaise of the personality. Even at his bleakest moments, Ronald clings to the idea of the good:

His melancholy and boredom returned with such force when he was alone again in his flat that he recited to himself as an exercise against it, a passage from the Epistle to the Philippians which was at present meaningless to his numb mind, in the sense that a coat of paint is meaningless to a window-frame, and yet both colours and preserves it: 'All that rings true, all that commands reverence, and all that makes for right; all that is pure, all that is lovely, all that is gracious in the telling; virtue and merit, wherever virtue and merit are found—let this be the argument of your thoughts' (p.116).

He also holds in mind the admirable qualities of others, though his honesty will not allow him to derive a sentimental comfort from these by submerging ugly attributes also discernible in his associates' personalities. Here, as before, truth is the quality Mrs Spark most highly values: conveying the intense importance of this by a scene where Ronald visits Elsie Forrest, hoping that she will return a stolen letter. Then an ethical duel occurs, with the attitude to life Mrs Spark endorses coming into conflict with that she dislikes, finds dangerous, and called in *The Ballad of Peckham Rye* 'Emotional'[18] morality. Elsie, lonely, eager for Ronald to become her lover or her friend, tries to use the letter as a weapon to manoeuvre him into involvement. With determined candour, however, he parries all her efforts:

'If I give you the letter now,' she said, 'will you come back again some time?'
'It's unlikely,' he said. 'You go to bed. Thank you for talking.'
'If I don't give you the letter what will you do?'
'I'll come back and try again.'
'Christ!' she said, 'you're driving me mad' (pp.183-4).

Earlier, too, Ronald has made a crucial distinction, saying of the letter:

'Give it to me for love.'
'What love do I get out of it?'
'That's not the point' (p.183).

Real love, he implies, is selfless; it is concerned with honesty, respect, refusal to pretend. In denying Elsie the spurious comforts she desires, comforts that in the long run will aggravate and not assuage her need—a temporary bed-companion, a 'friend' visiting her reluctantly and from a blackmail-coerced pity—he treats the girl with charity: and ultimately, strengthening her self-respect, this is to the good. It begins a process whereby, acting in the interests of the truth—exposing perjury and ensuring that Seton is convicted—she unknowingly saves the life of her friend, Alice.

This disinterested love, closely linked to truth and a respect for others' dignity, is surrounded in the novel by relationships in which the so-called love is false, thrown out of true, like the reflections in distorting mirrors, by irregular or twisted personalities: the affair of Isobel and Martin, with one partner swindling the other; Hildegarde's possessive love for Ronald; Mrs Bowles's suffocating mother-love; the 'love' Patrick directs at Freda Flower and at Alice. Loneliness—something Mrs Spark feels to be a serious contemporary affliction: 'Too many people suffer from boredom and loneliness. . . . I've known considerable loneliness. It's something I've written about and regard as a major problem of our society'[19]—is shown to panic people into meaningless allegiances, towards substitutes and compromise. But these are finally unsatisfactory, for from the inauthentic, Mrs Spark affirms, no good can come. Those who shut their eyes to truth, pretend that things are well when, manifestly, they are otherwise, only court, or cause, disaster. In that section of the book concerned with Lyte, Seton's half-accomplice in the plan to murder Alice, Mrs Spark, with skilled distaste, pins down the cowardly procedures of connivance, singling out and holding up to view the various constituents of moral decay: self-fostered ignorance, the carefully dulled conscience, the averted gaze. Frightened of past facts emerging, Lyte slides deeper into guilt, almost brings about a second death. Others, far less culpable but also stubbornly or timorously evasive, suffer the unpleasant repercussions for themselves. Freda Flower's hopeful gullibility soon squanders her savings; Elsie's half-wilful blindness lets Socket dupe away her time; Marlene Cooper's strained and strenuous optimism leaves her lonely and with no allies when the time of the trial comes; Isobel's uncritical dependence upon Martin gives him easy opportunity for knowledgeable pilfering; Alice's infatuated trust, determinedly defying evidence, all but ensures her destruction. Significantly, the moments in which there seems to be most love or intimacy in this novel are ones where truth is being communicated—scenes such as that between Ronald and Elsie, or between the two girls sitting in a darkening room:

> They sat hand-in-hand on the window seat and looked down on the lights of long Ebury Street.
> 'Yes,' Alice said, 'I suppose the main thing about Patrick is the talk.'
> 'Do you think he's going to marry you?'
> 'Of course. As soon as the divorce comes through.' . . .
> 'Aren't you afraid of Patrick?'
> 'Afraid? What is there to be afraid of?'
> 'Well, nothing that you know about. It's all the things you don't know about him. They say, about his forgeries—'
> 'Yes,' said Alice's voice in the dark, 'I'm afraid of the things I don't know. I don't want to know.'
> 'I feel the same,' Elsie said as she sat, almost invisible, 'about the Master' (pp.130–1).

Around these oasis moments of real contact, stretches a desert of monotony, urban cafard, boredom and solitude: a metropolitan wasteland swarming with hermits of circumstance. Satirically cataloguing separation, inability to make contact and the ills attendant on this—ostrich-like involvement with false friends, false lovers, false religion—*The Bachelors* is most appropriately set in 'London, the great city of bachelors' (p.1), the teeming, lonely capital, with its 'thirty-eight thousand five hundred streets, and seventeen point one bachelors to a street' (p.241). Effective enough in previous novels, the mise en scène is here drawn purposefully into the scheme of things, shown to have especial relevance: with the result that this book is a degree more tightly structured than its predecessors, where cohesion was largely achieved by a concentration upon people bonded together by some shared feature of their situation or their character: a tendency to *idées fixes*, traits of personality held oddly in common, extreme old age, reluctance to face truth. There is also in these works some degree of physical restriction, geographical line-drawing round the narrative: *The Comforters* is confined to Catholic or Bohemian enclaves of society, *Robinson* kept mainly to its desert island, *Memento Mori* to the wealthier boroughs of the capital, *The Ballad of Peckham Rye* to a poorer suburb, proletarian, south of the Thames. But in all these cases, the locale is not so firmly welded to the theme as it is in *The Bachelors* and will be more and more in later fictions. Part of Mrs Spark's economy is to insist increasingly upon concordance between the thesis of her book, its characters, and setting: and in *The Bachelors* this technique first comes to full maturity. There is—witty and serious like some conceit from Jacobean poetry—a constant correspondence between the mundane realities of celibacy, marriage, separation and divorce, and their metaphysical equivalents: creeds which attempt to keep separate, divorce the supernatural from the natural, or, favouring marriage and the sacramental, preach the indissoluble union of them. Ingeniously, the novel's celibates, portrayed with such sharp-eyed, sardonic zest, are made to stand as figures of its very abstract theme: the city in the background, where there is unnatural segregation on a massive scale, reinforcing this. Contingency is not despised. These people are offered for scrutiny amidst the accurately reproduced and idiosyncratic litter of their lives. The novel is stocked convincingly with informed detail from the worlds of medicine, spiritualism, law: its narrative generously thickened with comic particulars. But always relevance is felt, pulling the sprawl and tangle of reality into a clear design: so that, although the subjects of *The Bachelors* have failed to integrate, the book itself does so triumphantly. And in the next phase of her writing, aiming for even greater pertinence in all components of her fiction, Mrs Spark set out to work a further dimension—that of time—into the general accord.

4
Times Past

None of the various groupings into which the books of Muriel Spark can be arranged makes up so self-contained and tightly knit a unit as that consisting of *The Prime of Miss Jean Brodie*, *The Girls of Slender Means*, and *The Mandelbaum Gate*. Advancing chronologically through thirty years of this century, these novels are linked close by a chain of historical reaction. The events of the first book occur in silhouette against the rise of Fascism in Europe. The anti-Nazi struggle, culmination of this, closes as the second novel begins. The third, having at its core the trial of a war criminal, is largely set in Israel, a new state emerging from these earlier catastrophes and threatened now by impulses similar to those which generated them. Accordingly, the idea of group-pressure, chauvinistic membership of some community and what this can entail, is, in each novel, of considerable importance. Works too that have an obvious debt to autobiography—Mrs Spark was a schoolgirl in Edinburgh in the Thirties, lived in London at the end of World War II, and, half-Jewish like Barbara Vaughan, her heroine of *The Mandelbaum Gate*, visited Jerusalem during the Eichmann trial—these are three fictions that attempt 'to redeem the time',[1] to rescue the transient moment by lifting it from history's flux and giving it some aesthetic fixity. Extending the technique tentatively started in *The Comforters*, left aside for *Robinson*, and then developed through succeeding books, Mrs Spark now finds both periods and places that well match her themes. The settings of each novel, temporal and physical, local and political, lock together tightly to create a memorable symbol, an image—the élite group of a charismatic teacher in the Fascist Thirties; a hostel precariously surviving in impoverished London at the end of World War II; divided Jerusalem with the Eichmann trial proceeding—that, pinned down by sharp and salient detail, also provides the work's naturalistic geography. These, more than any other of her books, validate their author's claim: 'I think I am still a poet. I think my novels are the novels of a poet. I think like a poet and react as one.'[2]

The Prime of Miss Jean Brodie was the first of these fictions and like the second, its title—something of considerable significance for Mrs Spark: 'I always start with a title . . . and then work round different meanings. A novel is, for me, always an elaboration of a title'[3]—contains a play on words. 'Prime' as a noun—and it is used in this sense recurrently throughout the book—obviously refers to Miss Brodie's confident maturity. But the word can also be an adjective—a fact to which, at one point, attention is briefly drawn:

'She used to give us teas at her flat and tell us about her prime.'
'Prime what?' (p.31).[4]

And, in the sense of 'first', 'best', 'superior', it points to the centre of the novel and the set of chosen girls, potential candidates for 'life's élite or, as one might say, the crème de la crème' (p.27). Placed in Edinburgh, with most of its action confined to the nineteen-thirties, the book chronicles the rise and fall of a benevolent despot, a teacher who, as one of her pupils comes to recognize, is 'a born Fascist' (p.167). In the classroom at Marcia Blaine school, with Miss Brodie in command, elitism is passionately preached. Fervid allusions to the great, natural patricians splendidly exempt from mundane morality, pack the teacher's discourses. She talks of Cleopatra and Helen of Troy; the girls see her as Joan of Arc or some heroic Roman matron; Sybil Thorndike, Florence Nightingale, the Queen of England are held up as patterns of female nobility, whilst one 'term was filled with legends of Pavlova and her dedicated habits, her wild fits of temperament and her intolerance of the second-rate. "She screams at the chorus," said Miss Brodie, "which is permissible in a great artist" '(p.81). Nor is the pantheon solely stocked with women. Male idols are imported from the realm of politics. Miss Brodie is generous in reference to Mussolini—'one of the greatest men in the world, far more so than Ramsay MacDonald' (p.56); she holidays, with approval, in Italy—'Mussolini has performed feats of magnitude and unemployment is even farther abolished under him than it was last year' (p.57); and, on her return, decorates the classroom with propaganda pictures 'showing the triumphant march of the black uniforms in Rome' (p.38). Later, her adulation moves towards Hitler—'Miss Brodie . . . was going abroad, not to Italy this year but to Germany, where Hitler was become Chancellor, a prophet-figure like Thomas Carlyle, and more reliable than Mussolini; the German brownshirts, she said, were exactly the same as the Italian black, only more reliable' (p.130)—and to embattled Franco, a selected girl being urged to take up arms for him. And, as admiring Miss Brodie emulates her heroes, interesting parallels emerge. Enlarged and sinister like shadows on a backcloth, the Duce, Führer, and Caudillo show what is happening amongst the figures in the foreground. When, watching his *fascisti* march, Mussolini is described as standing 'on a platform like a gym teacher or a Guides mistress' (p.38), the simile is not simple deflation: for, as one of their number sees, the group of chosen girls are 'Miss Brodie's fascisti, not to the naked eye, marching along, but all knit together for her need and in another way, marching along' (p.38). The comparison bites two ways. Comically, the drilled warrior-elite resemble regimented schoolgirls: soberingly, children are being subjected to the accents and procedures of seductive tyranny. Events in Edinburgh stand as grimly witty analogues, different in scale but not in essence, to events in Europe. Miss Brodie's prime coincides with that of Fascism; her influence moves towards its zenith as the dictators extend their rule; her aims become more ruthless and corrupt as theirs do; she dies, 'the year after the war . . . from an internal growth' (p.72).

And, if the political climate of the book is perfectly adapted to its narrative, so is the religious atmosphere. The scene is Edinburgh, focal point of Calvinism, a creed which, also built around a concept of the chosen and the rejected, occupies a place in theology similar to that of Fascism in politics. St Giles Cathedral and the Tolbooth cast their premonitory gloom; the name of Knox sounds out; doctrines of predestination and divine election hover. Sandy, reading Calvin, finds he has 'made it God's pleasure to implant in certain people an erroneous sense of joy and salvation, so that their surprise at the end might be the nastier' (pp.144–5): and, as in weird parody, Miss Brodie's career exemplifies this. Like some justified sinner, she has 'elected herself to grace' (p.145) and this entails one of her pupils being declared 'predestined' (p.151) for the man she herself loves.

Miss Brodie's mind steeped in, her personality aligned towards, glamorous elitism, her teaching puts it into practice. 'Give me a girl,' she claims, 'at an impressionable age, and she is mine for life' (p.7): and six children chosen to be 'trained up in her confidence' (p.7) do become 'the corporate Brodie set' (p.51), their leader, after moments of doubt—'I sometimes fear it's too late, now. If you had been mine when you were seven you would have been the crème de la crème' (p.25)—declaring them to be 'mine . . . of my stamp and cut' (p.129). Even when officially no longer taught by her, the girls are kept within the sphere of influence: 'On most Saturday afternoons Miss Brodie entertained her old set to tea and listened to their new experiences. Herself, she told them, she did not think much of her new pupils' potentialities, and she described some of her new little girls and made the old ones laugh, which bound her set together more than ever and made them feel chosen' (p.104). Nor is the set simply an elite. Wisely, it also incorporates its ritual scapegoat, Mary Macgregor, 'famous for being stupid and always to blame' (p.13), 'officially the faulty one' (p.36): clumsy, dull, and culpable, predestined for chastisement, the Brodie Jew. Spilled ink (p.16) and damaged crockery (p.118) are automatically attributed to her; giggles provoked by the art-master tracing the curves of Botticelli ladies are quelled, almost ceremonially, by Mary's eviction (p.63). And the contagious viciousness inherent in this constant reaching for the branded victim is shown by the reponse of Sandy Stranger, shrewdest member of the group, when walking round the Old Town with Miss Brodie and her set:

> suddenly Sandy wanted to be kind to Mary Macgregor, and thought of the possibilities of feeling nice from being nice to Mary instead of blaming her. Miss Brodie's voice from behind was saying to Rose Stanley, 'You are all heroines in the making. Britain must be a fit country for heroines to live in. The League of Nations . . .' The sound of Miss Brodie's presence, just when it was on the tip of Sandy's tongue to be nice to Mary Macgregor, arrested the urge. Sandy looked back at her companions, and understood them as a body with Miss Brodie for the head. She perceived herself, the absent Jenny, the ever-blamed Mary, Rose, Eunice and Monica, all in a frightening little moment, in unified compliance to

the destiny of Miss Brodie, as if God had willed them to birth for that purpose.

She was even more frightened then, by her temptation to be nice to Mary Macgregor, since by this action she would separate herself, and be lonely, and blameable in a more dreadful way than Mary who, although officially the faulty one, was at least inside Miss Brodie's category of heroines in the making. So, for good fellowship's sake, Sandy said to Mary, 'I wouldn't be walking with *you* if Jenny was here' (pp.36-7).

This warping community-pressure is generated by Miss Brodie's unattractive attributes: contempt for the inferior, blind adulation of dictatorship: 'After the war Miss Brodie admitted to Sandy, as they sat in the Braid Hills Hotel, "Hitler *was* rather naughty," but at this time she was full of her travels and quite sure the new regime would save the world' (p.164). But the total portrait of the teacher is not one of simple condemnation. She is, it is stressed, victim as well as autocrat: partly a casualty of history. Just as Fascism sprouted from the aftermath of European conflict, so Miss Brodie's prime. Like Teddy Lloyd, who 'had lost the contents of [his] sleeve in the Great War' (p.61), she is war-deprived. Hugh, her fiancé, was killed in France, as she tells her class, children sitting under autumn trees and 'crying over history' (p.13): 'Season of mists and mellow fruitfulness. I was engaged to a young man at the beginning of the War but he fell on Flanders' Field. . . . He fell the week before Armistice was declared. He fell like an autumn leaf, although he was only twenty-two years of age' (pp.11-12). And in her loss and need to compensate for it, Miss Brodie is representative: 'There were legions of her kind during the nineteen-thirties, women from the age of thirty and upward, who crowded their war-bereaved spinsterhood with voyages of discovery into new ideas and energetic practices in art or social welfare, education or religion' (p.52). Sexual unrest, pangs of starved emotion are not the only forces fuelling Miss Brodie's missionary zeal, but they contribute potently to it. From time to time, romanticized response to foreign male allure tinges her travel-narratives of Italy—'I met a young poet by a fountain. Here is a picture of Dante meeting Beatrice' (p.58)—or Egypt— 'along the platform came my dragoman with a beautiful bunch of flowers for me. He had true dignity. . . . He was a very splendid person with a great sense of his bearing' (p.142). She is, as other teachers recognize, 'sex-bestirred' (p.60), sublimating restless impulses, first by a therapy-affair with unloved but suitably unmarried Mr Lowther; then, as her techniques and fantasies elaborate, by proxy, excitedly fostering involvement between the beauty of her set and the man she herself loves.

Here, as so often, however, life diverts her aims, reality travesties her schemes. Throughout the book—and it is another of the reasons why Miss Brodie does not finally leave a chilling impression—this is shown to happen. Her efforts to glue the girls together into a community are foredoomed, as early sections hint:

> The five girls, standing very close to each other because of the boys, wore their hats each with a definite difference.
> These girls formed the Brodie set (p.1);

and: 'The Brodie set smiled in understanding of various kinds' (p.7). Even as confining 'set' attempts to fasten them together, words like 'difference' and 'various' are unloosening the threads. Quietly, the linguistic structure indicates what is going to happen. Developing personalities will push Miss Brodie's influence aside; time and experience place her in a new perspective; the patterns she so eagerly anticipates are re-arranged by life; truth, it emerges, is much stranger than her fictions.

> It was plain that Miss Brodie wanted Rose with her instinct to start preparing to be Teddy Lloyd's lover, and Sandy with her insight to act as informant on the affair. . . . But in fact the art master's interest in Rose was simply a professional one, she was a good model; Rose had an instinct to be satisfied with this role, and in the event it was Sandy who slept with Teddy Lloyd and Rose who carried back the information (pp.145–6).

Only with Joyce Emily Hammond, the girl who was initially opposed to Franco, then inveigled into journeying to help him, does Miss Brodie succeed. And, even here, there is final failure in that—her train is attacked—the would-be recruit is killed before she can reach the Nationalists. For the rest, Miss Brodie's confident predictions fall in ruins:

> 'I am Gordon Lowther's closest friend, his confidante. I have neglected him of late I am afraid, but still I have been all things to Gordon Lowther, and I need only lift my little finger and he would be at my side. . . . I have had much calumny to put up with on account of my good offices at Cramond,' said Miss Brodie. 'However, I shall survive it. If I wished I could marry him tomorrow.'
>
> The morning after this saying, the engagement of Gordon Lowther to Miss Lockhart, the science teacher, was announced in *The Scotsman* (pp.150–1).

Her intentions buckle under pressures she has not envisaged; the ego-saturated atmosphere of infallibility—'She thinks she is Providence, thought Sandy, she thinks she is the God of Calvin, she sees the beginning and the end' (p.161)—is briskly dispelled by sharp gusts of reality. Not for nothing is *The Lady of Shalott*, with its tale of fantasy colliding fatally with fact, recited in the classroom.

But Miss Brodie does not fail entirely: and, in a sense, is only destroyed because she has succeeded. It may be true that Rose 'shook off Miss Brodie's influence as a dog shakes pond-water from its coat' (p.159); true that the teacher's efforts to manoeuvre people into liaisons satisfying to herself are arrogant, immoral, and, in any case, futile: but still the guarantee she gives her girls—'you will receive the fruits of my prime. They will remain with you all your days' (p.59)—is not without validity. Miss Brodie, despite her delusions and her mono-mania, is an inspiring teacher. The tone is comically egocentric:

> 'Who is the greatest Italian painter?'
> 'Leonardo da Vinci, Miss Brodie.'
> 'That is incorrect. The answer is Giotto, he is my favourite' (pp.9–10);

and the type of education offered is ludicrously at variance with that so vigorously defined:

> The word 'education' comes from the root *e* from *ex*, out, and *duco*, I lead. It means a leading out. To me education is a leading out of what is already there in the pupil's soul. To

77

Miss Mackay it is a putting in of something that is not there, and that is not what I call education. I call it intrusion, from the Latin root prefix *in* meaning in and the stem *trudo*, I thrust. Miss Mackay's method is to thrust a lot of information into the pupil's head; mine is a leading out of knowledge, and that is true education as is proved by the root meaning (p.45).

But, for all this, the result is 'not without its beneficent and enlarging effects' (p.114): pleasurable—even Mary Macgregor, looking back, feels that 'the first years with Miss Brodie, sitting listening to all those stories and opinions which had nothing to do with the ordinary world, had been the happiest time of her life' (p.15)—and valuable, implanting enthusiasm, promoting individuality. Miss Brodie, sarcastic on the subject of the team-spirit, may seem absurd, censure of group-loyalty coming oddly from the self-elected leader of a set. Yet what she says—'Ideas like "the team spirit". . . ought not to be enjoined on the female sex, especially if they are of that dedicated nature whose virtues from time immemorial have been utterly opposed to the concept' (p.103)—does point to the fatal contradiction in her purposes. She wants her girls to be both leaders and disciples, dominating others and subordinate to her: and, as events reveal, this is not possible. Earlier, too, gathering her elite, Miss Brodie has made an even more basic mistake. As the selected children grow towards the spectacular maturities prophesied for them, it becomes increasingly obvious that there is a gap between the vision and reality. These girls are not startlingly set apart from the common run of things: only one of them develops a dedicated nature opposed to the concept of the team-spirit; and it is because of this she brings about Miss Brodie's downfall.

This central figure is, of course, Sandy Stranger, through whose small eyes most of the events are witnessed, and in whom under Miss Brodie's shadow, a strong moral sense germinates, eventually supplanting the teacher. And the important element in Sandy's personality—one gradually pushing her towards ethical sensitivity—is her skill in reading art's coded communications. In this book, there are three main people who play serious games with reality, work it into shapes pleasing to themselves: Sandy, Miss Brodie, and Teddy Lloyd. Miss Brodie's fictions—at first, simple, naively romanticized accounts of dead Hugh, the soldier who 'fell like an autumn leaf' (p.12)— become, as her prime advances, increasingly complex, disingenuous, and oblique. The early lover, Sandy notices, is tricked out in attributes of more recent acquaintances:

> Miss Brodie's old love story was newly embroidered, under the elm, with curious threads: it appeared that while on leave from the war, her late fiancé had frequently taken her out sailing in a fishing boat and that they had spent some of their merriest times among the rocks and pebbles of a small seaport. 'Sometimes Hugh would sing, he had a rich tenor voice. At other times he fell silent and would set up his easel and paint. He was very talented at both arts, but I think the painter was the real Hugh.'
>
> This was the first time the girls had heard of Hugh's artistic leanings. Sandy puzzled over this and took counsel with Jenny, and it came to them both that Miss Brodie was making her new love story fit the old. Thereafter the two girls listened with double ears, and the rest of the class with single.
>
> Sandy was fascinated by this method of making patterns with facts, and was divided between her admiration for the technique and the pressing need to prove Miss Brodie guilty of misconduct (pp.93–4).

Obviously, the fiction here has become compensatory fantasy, as when Sandy, 'notorious for her small, almost non-existent, eyes' (p.4), attempts to remedy biology's injustices in the story she and Jenny write: ' "Never!" said Sandy, placing her young lithe body squarely in front of the latch and her arm through the bolt. Her large eyes flashed with an azure light of appeal' (p.21). This tale, the work of adolescents, is harmless, just as the fantasies the girls weave round their teacher are innocent enough. Significantly, as soon as Sandy feels they may be touching dangerous reality, she ends the pretence:

> 'Perhaps she's working it off on Mr. Lowther. Mr. Lowther isn't married.'
>
> It was a fantasy worked up between them, in defiance of Miss Gaunt and her forbidding brother, and it was understood in that way. But Sandy, remembering Miss Gaunt's

expression as she remarked 'It may be Miss Brodie has the same complaint as Mr. Lowther', was suddenly not sure that the suggestion was not true. For this reason she was more reticent than Jenny about the details of the imagined love affair. Jenny whispered, 'They go to bed. Then he puts out the light. Then their toes touch. And then Miss Brodie . . . Miss Brodie . . .' She broke into giggles.

'Miss Brodie yawns,' said Sandy in order to restore decency, now that she suspected it was all true (p.76).

For Miss Brodie, however, things are more serious. Whereas Sandy's fantasy-life largely derives from fiction—elaborations of *Kidnapped*, *Jane Eyre*, and *The Lady of Shalott* in which she participates with heady prominence—Miss Brodie tries to introduce fictional procedures into life, to treat the girls as if they were creations subject to her purposes: and this is in its turn reflected on the canvases of Teddy Lloyd where obsessively the pupils appear distorted into versions of their teacher, 'in a magical transfiguration, a different Jean Brodie under the forms of Rose, Sandy, Jenny, Mary, Monica and Eunice' (p.147).

It is Sandy's remarking of this and what it signifies, the way in which these girls are for the man not distinct individuals but mere ambassadors, Brodie tokens, that first pulls his interest towards her:

'It would be nice to do you all together,' he said, 'and see what sort of a group portrait I could make of you.'

Sandy thought this might be an attempt to keep the Brodie set together at the expense of the newly glimpsed individuality of its members. She turned on him in her new manner of sudden irritability and said, 'We'd look like one big Miss Brodie, I suppose.'

He laughed in a delighted way and looked at her more closely, as if for the first time. She looked back just as closely through her little eyes, with the near-blackmailing insolence of her knowledge. Whereupon he kissed her long and wetly. He said in his hoarse voice, 'That'll teach you to look at an artist like that' (pp.135–6).

The look has, however, been employed before:

'We told Miss Mackay how much you liked art,' said
Sandy. . . .

'I do indeed,' said Miss Brodie, 'but "like" is hardly the
word; pictorial art is my passion.'

'That's what I said,' said Sandy.

Miss Brodie looked at her as if to say, as in fact she had
said twice before, 'One day, Sandy, you will go too far for my
liking.'

'Compared to music,' said Sandy, blinking up at her with
her little pig-like eyes (p.86).

And in the case of both the painting and the myth-making, it is
thrift of procedure that first holds this unnerving attention:

Sandy was fascinated by the economy of Teddy Lloyd's
method, as she had been four years earlier by Miss Brodie's
variations on her love story. . . . Teddy Lloyd's method of
presentation was similar, it was economical, and it always
seemed afterwards to Sandy that where there was a choice of
various courses, the most economical was the best, and that
the course to be taken was the most expedient and most
suitable at the time for all the objects in hand. She acted on
this principle when the time came for her to betray Miss
Brodie (pp.134-5).

In fact, this time of betrayal arrives when Miss Brodie transfers
her dangerous flair from art to life: 'All at once Sandy realized
that this was not all theory and a kind of Brodie game, in the
way that so much of life was unreal talk and game-planning . . .
this was not theory; Miss Brodie meant it' (p.159). Quite
openly the teacher reveals that she regards her girls as little
more than marionettes, devoid of free will and individual value,
to be manoeuvred as her needs dictate:

'His portraits still resemble me?' said Miss Brodie.

'Yes, very much,' said Sandy.

'Then all is well,' said Miss Brodie. 'And after all, Sandy,'
she said, 'you are destined to be the great lover although I
would not have thought it. Truth is stranger than fiction.
I wanted Rose for him, I admit, and sometimes I regretted
urging young Joyce Emily to go to Spain to fight for Franco,
she would have done admirably for him, a girl of instinct,
a—' (p.165).

This is the speech, with its complete lack of awareness or regret, its blindness to everything but the self and its warped imperatives, that shows beyond doubt how the early romanticism has soured, fantasy hardened to psychosis. Before the process can begin again—Miss Brodie is already gathering another set around her—Sandy intervenes: and her main motive for doing so, for 'putting a stop to Miss Brodie' (p.167), is a moral one. She sees that the woman is betraying her pupils by treating them as objects—sexual delegates, convenient fodder for her political proclivities—and so is beyond the sphere of loyalty. But ironies still cling around the action. Sandy has, after all, been brought to her state of 'insight' and moral awareness, partly by Miss Brodie's process of 'putting old heads on . . . young shoulders' (p.6), and partly by recent exposure to the religion she has taken from the teacher's lover.

As this Catholicism grows increasingly important to her, she becomes a nun and, having witnessed a great deal of metamorphosis, achieved in art, attempted in life, takes as her new name 'Sister Helena of the Transfiguration', going on to write a 'strange book of psychology, "The Transfiguration of the Commonplace" ' (pp.170–1): a label which immediately adheres to Mrs Spark's procedures here. And, just in case the relevance is missed, the novel's closing lines draw fresh attention to it. Famous now for her book, Sandy is faced by an inquirer who asks:

> 'What were the main influences of your school days, Sister Helena? Were they literary or political or personal? Was it Calvinism?'
>
> Sandy said: 'There was a Miss Jean Brodie in her prime' (p.171).

With the novel in the background, the point is taken: Miss Brodie's influence is not an alternative to those the questioner suggests: it epitomizes all of them, the teacher being a pattern, her classroom a microcosm, by means of which conceptions such as Fascism or Calvinism are embodied, pushed into motion, scrutinized.

Elaborately worked into such figurations, the commonplace, the naturalistic layer of the fiction, is also vividly presented. Allegory has not bleached out detail. There is nothing palely generalized about the people or the setting of this book. Miss

Brodie is more than metaphor in a tweed coat. Edinburgh and Marcia Blaine School are not simply apt thematic-décor. The teacher who so dangerously confuses *duco* and *educo* is a convincing personality as well as an effective symbol. She is a recognizable figure at a particular moment in history, a comically and tragically deluded individual, a complex psychology where arrogance grows from frustration—'completely unrealized potentialities,' Mrs Spark has said, 'that's what Jean Brodie represents',[5] and hungrily all things—even one girl's vocation: 'Do you think she has done this to annoy me?' (p.82), and another's death: 'If this is a judgment on poor Mary for betraying me, I am sure I would not have wished . . .'(p.169)— are fed back to the starved self. The environment in which Miss Brodie moves is confidently realized: the school sketched in with a crisp authenticity: ink-spots dabbed from tussore silk blouses by the science mistress, *Tiger Tim's* torn up in disapproval, velours hats, a Latin folk-song, wind-swept hockey fields, a reproduction of the *Primavera*, a hundred lines of *Marmion*. There is verisimilitude as well as irony in Mrs Spark's depiction of the ambience and origins of the establishment:

> Marcia Blaine School for Girls was a day school which had been partially endowed in the middle of the nineteenth century by the wealthy widow of an Edinburgh bookbinder. She had been an admirer of Garibaldi before she died. Her manly portrait hung in the great hall, and was honoured every Founder's Day by a bunch of hard-wearing flowers such as chrysanthemums or dahlias. These were placed in a vase beneath the portrait, upon a lectern which also held an open Bible with the text underlined in red ink, 'O where shall I find a virtuous woman for her price is above rubies' (p.3).[6]

Her register of staff compresses documentary into sardonic cameo: dependable Miss Lockhart, the science teacher who could 'blow up the school with her jar of gunpowder and would never dream of doing so' (p.152); or, on the language side, 'A mademoiselle with black frizzy hair, who wore a striped shirt with real cuff-links . . . pronouncing French in a foreign way which never really caught on' (pp.99–100); and, of course, those many from the Junior School who 'stalked past Miss Brodie in the corridors saying "good morning" with predestination in their smiles' (p.99). The various stages of the girls' development towards maturity are carefully and accurately charted: wit here, as so frequently with this writer, astringently tightening observation. There is lively pastiche in Mrs Spark's retailing of the imaginary correspondence the schoolgirls concoct—'Allow me, in conclusion, to congratulate you warmly upon your sexual intercourse as well as your singing' (p.96)—but there is also seriousness, as for Sandy and Jenny this recreation is a means of fumbling towards a grasp of what is actually happening: 'I am dedicated to my Girls as is Madame Pavlova. . . . I may permit misconduct to occur again from time to time as an outlet because I am in my Prime' (pp.95–6). The comic muddle of Sunday newspaper sensation-drapery, romantic fiction cliché, and the inflated usages of formal letter-writing offers one kind of satisfaction. There is another in the way the girls' situation counterpoints that of their teacher—they moving through garbled fantasy about these things to realistic knowledge of them: she fast travelling out of reality and deeper into fantasy. Mrs Spark's power as symbolist is balanced by her ability to reproduce a scene compellingly. The Brodie set is an image, but, convincingly, the girls' different backgrounds, interests, futures are also written in. The city where they live is no mere 'time and landscape of the mind',[7] but Thirties Edinburgh, deftly evoked and briskly populated. Graphic vignettes display its social and topographical diversity; reference to the Fabians, the Idle, Marie Stopes, the Oxford Group hallmarks the period. A novel in whose genesis memory has obviously been a potent factor, *The Prime of Miss Jean Brodie* is the product of 'an exile in heart and mind—cautious, affectionate, critical':[8] and this equally applies to Mrs Spark's next book, *The Girls of Slender Means*.

Once again, the novel is partly a work of lovingly detailed reconstruction, a careful replica of the sight and sound of an era and an institution: this time, a girls' hostel in London between VE and VJ days. Austerity is now the note that dominates. It is a period when 'Everyone carried a shopping bag in case they should be lucky enough to pass a shop that had a sudden stock of something off the rations.' (p.3)[9] Food-queues form hopefully. Coupons are bartered. Clothes bear 'the utility-stamp, two half-moons facing the same way' (p.96). At an intellectual party, 'Beer was served in jam-jars, which was an affectation of the highest order, since jam-jars were at that time in shorter supply than glasses and mugs' (p.78). And this spare existence—it is 'the beginning of the hardest period of food-rationing, since the liberated countries had now to be supplied' (p.83)—stands revealed with especial clarity in the May of Teck Club: where the girls forage for soap, margarine and cold-cream, ingeniously improvise their clothes, share a Schiaparelli dress, try to economize on shillings for the meter, or cut down on the calorie-laden institutional meals. Thrift being a subject likely to call forth Mrs Spark's liveliest interest, all this is evoked with the usual vivid concision. But quickly, too, the book is moved away from documentary: shown to be much more than hard-edged illustration of the way we lived then. Its opening words—'Long ago in 1945' (p.1)—besides lightly stressing the gulf between contemporary life and that depicted here, are suitably fabular. Once again, Mrs Spark is writing not primarily as social chronicler but as 'an artist, a changer of actuality into something else'.[10] The historical trappings are being gathered for allegoric purposes. And again the title offers a convenient key to the workings of the novel.

It has, in fact, three distinct meanings, referring first and most obviously to the financial state of the club-members, their hostel having been established, as its Rules of Constitution state, 'for the Pecuniary Convenience and Social Protection of Ladies of Slender Means below the age of Thirty Years, who are obliged to reside apart from their Families in order to follow an Occupation in London' (p.4). The second connotation is, at least initially, comic—a joke that becomes serious: and relates to the fact that only the more slim-hipped of the girls—thirty-six and a quarter inches is the maximum—can squeeze out through the bathroom window to sunbathe on the roof. The third and last allusion, the most important though the least paraded, is to the meagre moral resources, the ethical impoverishment of these girls, as of all humanity. For some time, however, this interpretation is concealed, and the title merely seems to be a play on words, surreally coupling slimness of purse and hips, straitened circumstances and a narrow window. But that the hostel itself is to be viewed symbolically is rapidly ensured.

In this book, taking the covers from her allegorical procedures, Mrs Spark presents a character who does not simply talk—as Sandy Stranger did—about the transfiguration of the commonplace, but is shown attempting it. Nicholas Farringdon, a young writer struck by 'the beautiful aspects of poverty and charm amongst these girls' (p.74), finds himself increasingly attracted to the hostel and its way of life: 'This was a common effect of the May of Teck Club on its male visitors, and Nicholas was enamoured of the entity in only one exceptional way, that it stirred his poetic sense to a point of exasperation, for at the same time he discerned with irony the process of his own thoughts, how he was imposing upon this little society an image incomprehensible to itself' (p.89). Receiving from his first visit to the club 'a poetic image that teased his mind and pestered him for details' (p.80), Nicholas comes to see it as a pleasing embodiment of his utopian theories: 'a miniature expression of a free society . . . a community held together by the graceful attributes of a common poverty. He observed that at no point did poverty arrest the vitality of its members but rather nourished it. Poverty differs vastly from want, he thought' (pp.106–7). Yet, as he is also and self-mockingly aware, such mythologizing is comically remote from the way in which the girls themselves view their communal existence. Jane Wright, for instance, 'did not see the May of Teck Club as a mico-cosmic ideal society; far from it. The beautiful heedless poverty of a Golden Age did not come into the shilling-meter life which any sane girl would regard only as a temporary one until better opportunities occurred' (p.80). Despite this incongruity, how-ever, Nicholas persists in admiring the hostel as a working model of the creed outlined in his *Sabbath Notebooks*: 'We do not need a government. We do not need a House of Commons. Parliament should dissolve forever. We could manage very well in our movement towards a complete anarchist society, with our great but powerless institutions. . . . We do not need institutions with power. . . . We can be ruled by the corporate will of men's hearts alone' (p.70). Forgetting that it is a 'frozen image' (p.108), he ignores the factor, an essential one, that keeps it as it is: even though, earlier, he has heard quoted lines of Cavafy that encapsulate the situation—'and now what will become of us without Barbarians? Those people were some sort of a solution' (p.18).

Throughout the war, promoting internal co-operation within the menaced community, aggression has been channelled outwards, towards barbarians. Now, as external hostility declines—conflict in Europe ending as the narrative begins, that in Asia as it concludes—tensions and stress move inwards. With the thaw, dissensions start to crack a previously united nation. Victory in Europe is celebrated, and:

> The next day everyone began to consider where they personally stood in the new order of things.
>
> Many citizens felt the urge, which some began to indulge, to insult each other, in order to prove something or to test their ground (p.15).

Political rivalry, party conflict, begins again as the wartime coalition breaks apart: 'The wirelesses spoke forth their simultaneous Sinaitic predictions of what fate would befall the freedom-loving electorate should it vote for Labour in the forth-coming elections' (p.109). With the news of Hiroshima and the atom bomb, savagery no longer seems confined to the barbarians; and brutality is present too, violence shadowing the jubilation, in the picture of VJ night with which the novel ends: a woman knifed by a seaman; British and Americans, former allies, brawling in the park.

As the book progresses through its small but significant sector of history, symptoms of corruption thicken. Nicholas's confidence in the hostel as Arcadia is shaken by some of its members, thrifty in ways he cannot admire:

> The weeks had passed, and since in the May of Teck Club they were weeks of youth in the ethos of war, they were capable of accommodating quick happenings and reversals, rapid formations of intimate friendships, and a range of lost and discovered loves that in later life and in peace would take years to happen, grow and fade. The May of Teck girls were nothing if not economical. Nicholas, who was past his youth, was shocked at heart by their week-by-week emotions.
>
> 'I thought you said she was in love with the boy.'
>
> 'So she was.'
>
> 'Well, wasn't it only last week he died? You said he died of dysentery in Burma.'
>
> 'Yes, I know. But she met this naval type on Monday, she's madly in love with him.'
>
> 'She can't be in love with him,' said Nicholas.

'Well, they've got a lot in common she says.'
'A lot in common? It's only Wednesday now' (pp.120–1).

After which, precisely on cue, the voice of Joanna is heard declaiming from *The Ancient Mariner*:

> Like one, that on a lonesome road
> Doth walk in fear and dread,
> And having once turned round, walks on,
> And turns no more his head;
> Because he knows a frightful fiend
> Doth close behind him tread (p.121).

And the relevance is not hard to take. The spectre Nicholas fears to face is that of man's imperfection. Determinedly oblivious instead, he stays close to his view of the hostel as streamlined utopia—non-proprietary, harmoniously communal —even extending his symbol-making to include Selina:

> With the reckless ambition of a visionary, he pushed his passion for Selina into a desire that she, too, should accept and exploit the outlines of poverty in her life. He loved her as he loved his native country. He wanted Selina to be an ideal society personified amongst her bones, he wanted her beautiful limbs to obey her mind and heart like intelligent men and women, and for these to possess the same grace and beauty as her body. . . . It was incredible to him that she should not share with him an understanding of the lovely attributes of dispossession and poverty, her body was so austere and economically furnished (pp.116–7).

In his idealizing of the girl, however—with whom he makes love on the hostel roof, economically slaking two infatuations— he is even further from reality than in his idealizing of the institution. Selina, as events increasingly reveal, is not simply unaware of poverty's charm, oblivious to the joys of responsible community: she is acquisitive, unscrupulous, intensely self-regarding. And it is through her that Nicholas is finally made to see his error: on the night of the fire, as the hostel, his image, is consumed by flames.

Easily escaping from the burning building, Selina turns and makes her poised way back through trapped friends and companions, to rescue a dress. 'It was hell,' (p.180) says one of the girls after this: and the implication, though laid into place with a characteristically light touch, is very serious, for Nicholas, who has written that 'a vision of evil may be as effective to conversion as a vision of good' (p.180), sees in Selina's callous rapacity an 'action of savagery so extreme that it forced him involuntarily to make an unaccustomed gesture, the signing of the cross upon himself' (p.73). The fire 'probably turned his brain' (p.149), a character later remarks: and, in a sense other than she intends, it is shown to have done so. Initially, stress has fallen upon Nicholas's wavering, his lack of direction:

he had been always undecided whether to live in England or France, and whether he preferred men or women, since he alternated between passionate intervals with both. Also, he could never make up his mind between suicide and an equally drastic course of action known as Father D'Arcy. Rudi explained that the latter was a Jesuit philosopher who had the monopoly for converting the English intellectuals. Nicholas was a pacifist up to the outbreak of war, Rudi said, then he joined the army (p.63).

Then, harshly, he is taught the precariousness of decency, sees the girl he loves behaving with voracity and total self-concern, as his whole idealized structure collapses: and

'Is it safe out here?' said Selina.
'Nowhere's safe,' said Nicholas (p.161).

Acting as searing illustration of what he has earlier stated: 'Everyone should be persuaded to remember how far, and with what a pathetic thump, the world has fallen from grace' (p.68), this spectacle galvanizes Nicholas' religious sense, fixes his life. The destruction of the May of Teck—as a result of the belated detonation of explosive potential long latent and ignored at its foundation—displays the futility of man's efforts to live communally without aggressive competition. The paradisal commune of Nicholas' anarchist theories is doomed because it is based on purely human resources. 'Except the Lord build the house: their labour is but lost that build it' (p.164), Joanna is reciting just before her death: and the annihilation of the hostel—where the poverty has been unavoidable, not voluntary as in a religious community: endured rather than chosen—is meant to emphasize this point.

It also serves to illustrate another concept, the novel's references to *The Wreck of the Deutschland* here becoming pertinent. The circumstances of Joanna's death, it is noticeable, closely resemble those of the nun in that poem. In both cases, a figure of integrity about to die violently becomes the focus of appalled attention: and in both cases, too, the explanation offered for the tragedy is that God educates through dread:

> The frown of his face
> Before me, the hurtle of hell
> Behind, where, where was a, where was a place? (p.20)

Like Hopkins, Nicholas contemplates the horrible destruction of the good—for, far more than her convenience as mouthpiece for those lines of verse that ring so appositely through the May of Teck, Joanna is important as counter-figure to Selina. 'I'm shockable' (p.132), she meekly admits at one point in the novel; her ruling characteristic is what Jane thinks of as 'Joanna's disinterestedness, her ability, a gift, to forget herself and her personality' (p.143): and all of this is obviously antithetical to those standards enshrined in the Two Sentences: 'Poise is perfect balance, an equanimity of body and mind, complete composure whatever the social scene. Elegant dress, immaculate grooming, and perfect deportment all contribute to the attainment of self-confidence' (pp.59–60). These—poise, balance, equanimity, composure—are qualities Mrs Spark distrusts as breeding egoism and complacency. Her most admirable characters are never the self-confident, but the self-mocking, the self-questioning, or self-forgetting. Her fiction is much concerned with shaking assurance, dealing out morally therapeutic shocks—of the kind adminstered to Nicholas in this book by the exploding bomb. And, certainly, in his case, the effects are to be seen as ultimately beneficial. Starkly illuminating life's realities, the disaster dispels his fantasies. He watches unselfishness fall to the flames while selfishness escapes: and the glimpse, at this traumatic time, of ugly impulses behind Selina's beauty shows too how he has misled himself into a facile equation of the ethical and the aesthetic, sentimentally assuming that physical and moral grace would necessarily exist together, the one figuring the other.

After these events, as the book's last lines make clear, he comes to see things in a new perspective and to recognize that neither Joanna, displaying the best qualities, nor Selina, displaying the worst, truly represents the spirit of the hostel: but that it is Jane, with her dogged and unglamorous determination to push on, who provides its real epitome:

> Jane mumbled, 'Well, I wouldn't have missed it, really.' She had halted to pin up her straggling hair, and had a hairpin in her mouth as she said it. Nicholas marvelled at her stamina, recalling her in this image years later in the country of his death—how she stood, sturdy and bare-legged on the dark grass, occupied with her hair—as if this was an image of all the May of Teck establishment in its meek, unselfconscious attitudes of poverty, long ago in 1945 (p.183).

Like Dougal Douglas, Ronald Bridges, Sandy Stranger, Nicholas, besides playing a crucial role in the narrative, is thriftily put to performing some of the author's work for her. Through him, Mrs Spark isolates and illustrates that most constant factor of her fictional technique: the turning of a very small community into an image. The two may differ in their evaluation of the May of Teck—Nicholas at first taking it to show the attractive possibility of a society governed solely by man's better instincts: Mrs Spark using it to prove the impossibility of this for more than a short and special period of time, when the grimmer impulses are busy looking outwards. But in their eagerness to create symbol, they are very similar. Nicholas's cohesive responses:

> The sounds and sights impinging on him from the hall of the club intensified themselves, whenever he called, into one sensation, as if with a will of their own. He thought of the lines:
>
>> Let us roll all our strength, and all
>> Our sweetness up into one ball (p.106),

his pulling of all externals back towards an allegoric core, parallel some of Mrs Spark's reactions and her basic strategy. But he does not, of course, encompass everything she offers as a novelist. Actuality here, as generally in her writing, is not simply transfigured: it is also richly present.

Twice in the book a snatch of song is caught on the wireless:

> There were angels dining at the Ritz
> And a nightingale sang in Berkeley Square (pp. 58, 142).

And this is more than period wallpaper, of a piece with reference to Jack Buchanan, Bertorelli's, or The Wheatsheaf. Lyrically, it summarizes the procedure of the novel and indeed of almost all Mrs Spark's writing: the way that trivia and significance are coupled, the contingent and the necessary—the Ritz and angels, Berkeley Square and a symbolic nightingale—brought inextricably together. This fusion is what gives her work its distinctive quality. Attempting authorship in *The Prime of Miss Jean Brodie*, Sandy and Jenny were said to be faced with the problem of presenting their teacher in both a favourable and unfavourable light. It was a problem Mrs Spark also had to face in that novel: but the more demanding task she has continually had to tackle in her writing is how to present a community both seriously and comically, how to reconcile the strict formal pleasures of allegory with the more discursive satisfactions of satiric documentary. Her solution has been by skilled economy—ordering her drily amused perceptions into didactic pattern, ensuring that the counters of her parables are not block-capitalled as to what they represent but alive with witty detail. The gargoyles, whenever possible, are functional, part of the structure. Most components of her fiction serve several purposes: and this applies especially to the characters. Nicholas in this novel, for instance, is not merely a symbolist who represents one of the author's favourite techniques, not merely idealism looking for a satisfactory object, but on the social level a convincingly presented individual in accurately drawn surroundings, an amateur poet and anarchist, something which blends well into the period setting, opens opportunities for satire (as at the intellectual party he attends with Jane), and connects importantly with the novel's theme. Selina, whose confidence in herself both neatly parallels Nicholas' more generalized confidence in human nature and finally shatters it, is no poster-blatant Egoism from a crude morality, but a solid and detailed personality built up by an accretion of revealing traits: addiction to charm-school runes, preference for vulnerable men, langorous assertion through physical endowment—'she lolled in the distinct attitude of being the only one present who could afford to loll' (p.49). Joanna, too, is used to multiple effect. Exemplifying unselfishness, she is still not simplified or exempted from that ironic scrutiny Mrs Spark directs at all her characters. In the work's allegoric pattern, Joanna figures as meek and destroyed virtue. The pervasively satiric atmosphere ensures that she also receives her share of sardonic commentary as one who lacks experience, is emotionally immature (it is perhaps not accidental that her surname is Childe), and has been innocently conditioned by the part-absurd, part-admirable ideals of a very specific ethos.

Mrs Spark's ability to extract as much as possible from each section of her novel is well demonstrated by the scene in which Joanna listens to a sermon by the curate she is deciding to renounce. Basically, this illustrates the unwordly and naive conventions worked into her moral system by her rectory upbringing: 'Once you admit that you can change the object of a strongly-felt affection, you undermine the whole structure of love and marriage . . . this had been the approved, though unspoken, opinion of the rectory, and its mental acres of upper air' (p.22). But there are other things happening at the same time. The chosen text is: '. . . if thy right eye offend thee, pluck it out, and cast it from thee: for it is profitable for thee that one of thy members should perish and not that thy whole body should be cast into hell' (p.23). This provides comedy as the curate, hoping to impress Joanna, unwittingly preaches himself out of her life: 'Joanna listened attentively to the young man in the pulpit, she listened obsessively. . . . The right eye and the right hand, he was saying, means that which we hold most precious. . . . Joanna decided to pluck out her right eye, cut off her right hand, this looming offence to the first love, this stumbling block, the adorable man in the pulpit' (p.24). It also points forward to the situation of Nicholas who, having seen one member perish but the body survive, on the night of the hostel fire, will avoid the smart hell Selina inhabits, renounce what he has held precious, and enter very maimed into the kingdom of heaven.

The verse Joanna is given to reciting is another instance of this fruitful artistic parsimony. Sufficiently declamatory in mode to suit the needs of an elocution teacher and to reveal the girl's repressed emotionalism, many of these extracts serve the additional purpose of elaborating or stressing the novel's main concerns. Lines from *Dover Beach* lament the decline of faith. Fragments of the *Ode to the West Wind* bring the idea of preservation through destruction to the fore, death as a necessary prelude to rebirth:

> Drive my dead thoughts over the universe
> Like withered leaves to quicken a new birth! (p.142).

Moonlit Apples touches on the idea of ripening immaturity. A couplet from Auden's *Lullaby*, one of the few contemporary poems to have the vibrancy that so appeals to Joanna:

> Lay your sleeping head, my love,
> Human on my faithless arm (p.7)

draws a ring around that human fallibility with which the novel is concerned. Quotations from Wordsworth's *Resolution and Independence* signpost the way Nicholas is to take from delight in humanity to disillusion with it:

> By our own spirits are we deified:
> We Poets in our youth begin in gladness;
> But thereof come in the end despondency and madness (p.49):

and *The Wreck of the Deutschland*, pervading the book, explains why he will do so.

Relevance controls the work. Wherever possible, its gaudy instances of life's variety are firmly anchored to the theme. Jane's hopeful correspondence with the famed gives splendid scope for literary pastiche. 'Thank you for your letter in praise of my writings. As you say they have consoled you in your misfortunes, I shall not attempt to gild the lily by my personal comments. As you say you desire no money I shall not press upon you my holograph signature which has some cash value. G.B.S.' (pp.56–7). It is also perfectly in keeping with the book's concerns, as this activity stems from the poverty in which she lives. Much comic energy goes into the creation of the hostel, but we are never allowed to lose sight of its real significance behind the vivid layer that records quotidian absurdity. There is in the novel a most satisfactory interplay, each helping the other, between symbol and mocking depiction. Events trivial at first glance are used to spell out absolutes: and these same absolutes throw a derisive shadow on the everyday. From her raw material here, Mrs Spark, with economic flair, makes both allegoric capital and satiric interest.

A further bonus is her style, healthily full of unexpected aptnesses: fat Jane spending time 'in eager dread of the next meal' (p.36); a man described as 'orthosexual', the joke being that—normally clashing prefixes falling oddly into concord—this means heterosexual. Metaphor is used to staple character memorably in place: ' "Christianity is all in the country parishes these days," said this shepherd of the best prime mutton' (p.172). Simile ties mockingly pictorial labels on to personality: 'Dorothy Markham, the chattering débutante whose bright life, for the past forty-three minutes, had gone into a bewildering darkness like illuminations at a seaside town when the electricity system breaks down' (p.165). As usual, Mrs Spark shows her radar ability to pick up the symptomatic turn of phrase: 'On these evenings of no guests the members . . . were reminded that they were expected to put everything back in place after a dance had been held in the club. Why some members unfortunately just went off to night clubs with their men friends and left everything to others, said the warden, she simply did not know' (p.35); or the epitomizing gesture: 'The clergyman signed irritably with his hand to convey the moment when the drink was to his taste. He had the mannerisms of a widower of long years, or of one unaccustomed to being in the company of critical women' (p.170). Briskly and with exhilarating accuracy she follows the devious twists of psychology—as when Jane feels she has betrayed George:

she gazed at the letter she had written and wondered what to do about her feelings. She decided to telephone to his wife, Tilly, and have a friendly chat about something. . . . Jane was usually bored by Tilly. . . . But her heart in its treachery now swelled with an access of warmth for Tilly. She telephoned and invited her to supper on Friday. Jane had already calculated that if Tilly should be a complete bore, they would be able to fill in an hour with Mrs. G. Felix Dobell's lecture. . . . "There's a talk on Friday by an American woman on the Western Woman's Mission, but we won't listen to that, it would be a bore." Jane said, contradicting her resolution in her effusive anxiety to sacrifice anything, anything to George's wife, now that she had betrayed and was about to deceive George' (pp.129–30).

Moral documentation of this kind is, in its witty authenticity, already pleasurable enough: but Mrs Spark, unwilling to leave any jagged pieces, makes it serve a purpose in the narrative as well. Jane's guilt-edged invitation is accepted eagerly: 'Tilly said, "I always love the May of Teck. It's like being back at school." Tilly always said that, it was infuriating' (p.130). Returning to the club on Friday evening, Jane is met by a scream from the top floor, a false prelude, it turns out, to a real tragedy. This scream merely signals that Tilly is wedged in the bathroom window—' "She said it was like being back at school, here in the club," Anne Baberton explains, "so Selina showed her the window" ' (p.138)—but, before the chapter ends, more serious screaming is heard and the ability to slide through this window has become a matter of life or death. In its sounding of the alarm—'A scream of panic from the top floor penetrated the house' (p.137) is the chapter's opening line—only to let this lapse in bathos so the reader lowers his guard before the true attack is launched, this device and its effect are best summed up perhaps by an image from Mrs Spark's next book, *The Mandelbaum Gate*: 'the sensation of one who has had a disturbing dream, the culmination of which was the ringing of a telephone, and wakes with relief to discover the telephone is in fact ringing beside his bed, and answers it, only to hear disturbing news.'[11]

Fictional carpentry like this, incident dovetailing into incident so that the eye and mind are effortlessly drawn on, combines with the novel's high degree of surface polish and its clean-lined structure—most elements, however ornamental they at first appear, turning out to be ingeniously functional—to place *The Girls of Slender Means* alongside *The Prime of Miss Jean Brodie* as Muriel Spark's finest achievement in transfiguring the commonplace. The tension between pleasure and morality, life and image, character as psychological or social portrait and character as unit of allegory is here impressively maintained without either side incurring damage. In these works, actuality and pattern beautifully synchronize, the formal and naturalistic coexist without distorting strain. After them— perhaps feeling these fictions to be the farthest she could go in that particular direction; perhaps unhappy about the way they

were, for all their grim concerns, still largely received as rather
flippant entertainment—Mrs Spark begins increasingly to
experiment, to modify the fictional prototype she had been
refining now through six of her novels.

While working on the book that became *The Mandelbaum
Gate*, for instance, she said in a television interview, 'this is the
first time that I'm hoping to do a new form of novel':[12] and
went on to explain that it was to be heavily autobiographical,
an account of three generations of women—she herself, her
mother, and her grandmother—and would be called *The
Gentile Jewess*. Part of this original version finally saw the light
as a short story of the same name.[13] But the novel as we now
have it is something very different. Much of the material
intended for *The Gentile Jewess* has presumably been worked
into those sections of the book concerned with Barbara
Vaughan. The technique, however, is not at all like that first-
person, autobiographical mode employed for the earlier draft.
Innovation in *The Mandelbaum Gate*, in fact, basically consists
of a magnification of those procedures put to such good effect
in the two previous books. There is a great enlargement of
scale. Mrs. Spark works on a bigger canvas and, at the same
time, uses smaller strokes.

As its title would suggest, the novel deals with division, most
of its events taking place in or around the bisected Jerusalem of
1961: a partitioned city where the Mandelbaum Gate—'hardly
a gate at all, but a piece of street between Jerusalem and
Jerusalem, flanked by two huts, and called by that name
because a house at the other end once belonged to a Mr.
Mandelbaum' (p.330)[14]—acts as crossing-point 'from Jerusalem to Jerusalem' (p.4). This basic severance, an absurd
dividing-line slicing through obvious unity, displays the novel's
motif in its simplest, crudest, most dramatic form. Around it,
elaborating this, stretches a vast web of wide or hair-line
fracture. Jerusalem, it rapidly emerges, is not simply cleft in
two: it is fragmented. The larger hostile factions, Arab-Jew,
Christian-Muslim, are themselves internally splintered by
dissent, group-schism, sect-enthusiasm. Each cell of bigotry
breaks down into smaller cells, insulated, in their turn, behind
impermeable layers of prejudice. Centre of the Holy Land,
Jerusalem is notoriously pulled apart by differing religious

creeds: mosques, synagogues, and churches jostle in its streets. But this tripartite split, immediately visible, is only a beginning. Within each allegiance are antagonistic subdivisions—as Mrs Spark crisply conveys by a scene in the Church of the Holy Sepulchre, a major Christian shrine and battleground for piously contending sects:

> At the other altar in the chapel the Greek rite proceeded under the equally jealous eyes of its custodians, and the chanting murmur of the Orthodox responses droned busily about the ears of the Latin persuasion, so that the blessed mutter of the Roman Mass could scarcely be heard by the faithful; the Franciscans were accustomed to this and were aware that nothing could be done about it. It was true that from time to time feelings came to a boil, and a quarrel would take place between the subordinate brothers of either communion, not to mention the words that had been known to arise when the Copts, Syrians, or even the Gregorian Armenians overstepped the mark on the sacred site of the death, burial, and resurrection of the Saviour (p.209).

Other varieties of Christian dissent are drawn into the picture by the fact that the attendant Franciscans, once rebuked for kneeling to kiss the ring of 'the Schismatic of Canterbury' (p.213), are now outraged by the sermon of a fellow-Catholic priest versed in more contemporary theology than theirs. Highly ecumenical, 'One of the new upstarts; comparing Moslems to good Catholics in the same breath' (p.211), he provokes an indignation that is largely doctrinaire, but contains, too, its trace of nationalist inflammability: 'the friars stood mute, with downcast eyes, content to wait for their justification in Heaven, which, being all Italian territory, would be so ordered that foreign firebrands like this one would be kept firmly in their place' (p.215).

Even amongst the members of an ostensible alliance, the book continually points out, bigotry puts up its fences. And, of course, it is not only Christianity that is so divided: orthodox and unorthodox Jewish sects are also shown mutually disapproving. Nor is it just religious faiths that crumble down into competing factions. Political confederations likewise consist of precariously-held-together particles, as Abdul's experience exemplifies:

It made him feel good to belong to an Arab movement. He liked to feel that it was something to be an Arab, although he disliked the Lebanese and wished all the Arabs were Palestinian or Transjordanian, and less alien in their ways. Abdul's teacher in history, a Syrian, was pro-Hitler. Another of the teachers, an English communist, was the guiding spirit of another student faction. The cells split open from time to time, forming themselves anew, after some shouting, fighting, and expulsions of students, into regional structures, so that the Lebanese, the Egyptians, the Tunisians, Arabians and Syrians were plotters in separate fields of political allegiance. Every man among the Arab students proclaimed himself a nationalist, this word being their only common denominator (p.97).

On closer scrutiny, each large bloc, whether religious, racial, or political, turns out to be a very shaky unit, shows a network of cracks. These fragmenting lines, however—life-or-death distinctions to heated partisans—dwindle into insignificance when seen in more remote perspective. To the Western eyes of Jerusalem's English colony, Arab and Jew can be physically indistinguishable: 'The man said something in Arabic. Freddy had thought he was a Jew. You couldn't tell the difference sometimes' (p.15). For them, the struggle in Palestine is merely 'a blood-feud between Semites' (p.79), like fighting like, the antagonists, whatever their declared differences, all really bunched together as fiery Middle Eastern foreigners. Assembling in 'a delightful English atmosphere' (p.65), on 'an island of mutual Englishness' (p.76), the diplomats, relief workers, and tourists generally exercise a milder form of prejudice than most of that raging around them, but are still susceptible to the cosy warmth of shared contempt, capable of surrendering their individuality to freemasonry's heartening complacencies. Thus, Freddy Hamilton and Barbara Vaughan, embarrassingly divided by a social awkwardness, can quickly reunite in 'an English giggle' (p.14) about the comic native lack of savoir-faire: ice-cubes dissolving into lukewarm wine. 'They simply don't understand about wine at most of these hotels' (p.14), sighs Freddy: and the seigneurial pronoun, with its holding at arm's length, rings confidently through English reaction to the Middle East and its inhabitants—'Freddy bumped into a man in European dress, rushing out of a shop as they all did' (p.5), 'they were all apt to get intense' (p.9), 'They think in symbols. . . . And when they speak in symbols it sounds like lies' (p.67).

These transients in Palestine also introduce a distinctively English brand of divisiveness into the book's compendium of apartheids: that of class distinction. Reflex sensitivity to this is seen from time to time in upper-class Freddy, whose letters to Harrogate make clear: 'The Eichmann who is on trial here in Jerusalem is an inferior sort of person with no connections whatsoever. I believe his antecedents are quite obscure' (p.92). But it is most pervasive in those scenes that flash-back to England and spotlight the reactions of Barbara's cousins, 'gaily mimicking Harry's Coventry vowels' (p.41), to Clegg, the archaeologist with whom she is in love: 'They conveyed, with innocent remarks, in their diffident way, their amusement at the points where his lower-class origins were evident' (p.37). Generally less virulent than religious or political animosity, class still digs its dividing ditches: and so, as Mrs Spark goes on to show, does 'type'. Complacently regarding Barbara as sexless bluestocking and Clegg—'not their type socially' (p.37) —as comic boffin:

> Miles and Kathy merrily departed for dinner parties, leaving the professor baby-sitting with Barbara and presumably discussing archaeology with her for all he was worth.
> But Barbara and Harry Clegg were in the spare bedroom, making love (p.37).

For Mrs Spark, such social myopia is culpable. Unwilling to tackle the difficulty and complexity of the individual, attention, she stresses, is lazily prone to stop short at the type with its comfortingly familiar features. And Barbara, 'the safe type' (p.75), thinks of this with indignation as she leaves the convent in Jordan:

> Immediately on passing into the night air she realized that she had almost hoped to be caught, it would have been a relief and a kind of triumph and justification. For there had been a decided element of false assumption in her reception at the convent the previous day, after they had inquired politely, and estimated her type. Of course she was an English

Catholic convert. She was indeed the quiet type. But there was a lot more than met the eye, at least she hoped so. She had thought, as the Mother Superior made her benign speech of welcome, and the old Novice-mistress hovered with an admiring smile, if only they knew. And she was inwardly exasperated, as she had been with her cousins last summer, when she had carried on a love-affair with Harry Clegg, there in the house, and they, in their smug insolence, had failed to discover it. And why? She thought now, with the old exasperation, what right have they to take me at my face value? Every spinster should be assumed guilty before she is proved innocent, it is only common civility. People, she thought, believe what they want to believe; anything rather than shake up their ideas (p.160).

The novel swarms with instances of people believing what they want to believe, thinking in terms of type not person, the species rather than the individual, and then going on to regard these different groups or categories as alien, potentially or actually hostile. Obviously, ethos, tradition, and environment must to some extent colour those steeped in them: Freddy has the family trait of shunning taxis; Alexandros, an ancestral reluctance to miss making a sale; at Passover, the independent-minded Aaronsons 'were suddenly children of Israel again' (p.30); and as emancipated Abdul and Mendel greet each other: 'The courteous contours of the old language half-imposed themselves on these preludes to their conversation, sentence by sentence, as if tradition itself were fumbling its way among the aberrant communications of the two men' (p.110). But the important thing is to look past these external insignia,[15] to realize that, as Barbara declares: 'There's always more to it then Jew, Gentile, half-Jew, half-Gentile. There's the human soul, the individual. Not "Jew, Gentile" as one might say "autumn, winter". Something unique and unrepeatable' (p.34).

The danger in this novel, as usual in Mrs Spark's fiction, comes from mental sloth and hazily emotional response, a trading in simplicities, refusal to face fact. These are the things which create the absurd divisions and dichotomies that everywhere zigzag their way across Jerusalem. The barriers are put up by dishonesty; they are arbitrary; reality in no way corresponds to these simplistic boundaries marked out across it, as Mrs Spark repeatedly illustrates:

> The night now began to give out the chanting of the minarets, from Israel across the border to the west of the convent, then nearer, to the north, from the direction of the Holy Sepulchre. It was three o'clock. The chanting voices echoed each other from height to height like the mating cries of sublime eagles. . . . From the east, beyond the Wailing Wall, a white-clad figure raised his arms in the moonlight and now began his call to prayer, and soon, from far in the south, then in the south-east, and from everywhere, the cry was raised (p.155).

The Wailing Wall, a Jewish place of pilgrimage, and the Holy Sepulchre, a Christian one, are on the Arab side of the Gate: the muezzin's call to prayer goes up from Israel as well as Jordan. Throughout Palestine, too, defying demarcation, thrive flowers and herbs 'recognizable to Freddy as belonging to the same botanical tribes as the wild flowers of the English fields and hedgerows of his schooldays before everything had been changed' (p.49) and:

> Their seeds had been brought to Palestine and sown, he suspected, by a conspiracy of the English Spinster under the Mandate. A second cousin of his had done the same service for India, where she had returned after every home leave with a shoe-box full of wild flowers gone to seed. This virgin cousin had expressed the sentiment that when she scattered these flowers abroad in the fields and side-walks of India, she was doing something to unite East and West. Her father had shouted her down, in his fierce manner, denouncing the practice. 'Never the twain shall meet—' he reminded her, as if the words were Holy Writ. The old brigadier had gone on to tell Cousin Beryl that she was only making a lot of damn difficulties for the botanists; he added—irrelevantly as it had seemed at the time—that he himself had once forbidden an Indian servant to marry a girl from Bhutan, because it would only lead to a damn muddle in the offspring (p.53).

As this extract shows, Mrs Spark is continually extending her map of division. Without any effect of strain, she covers the whole span of prejudice. Running its ugly course at the heart of Israel, the Eichmann trial gives a glimpse of category-hatred carried to the limit: attempted genocide, the mass extermination of those labelled racial dross. Bigotry here is at the farthest possible remove from the individual; the concern is all with species. And the intolerance is totally depersonalized, mechanized into a streamlined massacre: 'I was concerned strictly with time-tables and technical transport problems' (p.188). This—Eichmann in his glass cell, listening to a bureaucratic litany of slaughter—is one end of the spectrum. At the other, Mrs Spark places moments where, almost unthinkingly, bias flickers forth among people who are usually tolerant, rational, and courteous. Talking with Freddy, Barbara remarks that Jews:

> believe with their blood. Being a Jew isn't something they consider in their minds, weigh up, and give assent to as one does in the Western Christian tradition. Being a Jew is inherent.
>
> 'Yes, I'm afraid so', Freddy gave a little laugh.
>
> As if he had not spoken at all, she continued, 'As a half-Jew myself, I think I understand how—'
>
> 'Oh, I didn't mean to say . . . I mean . . . One says things without thinking, you know.'
>
> She said, 'You might have said worse.'
>
> Freddy felt terrible. He groped for the idea that, being a half-Jew, she might be only half-offended. After all, one might speak in that manner of the Wogs or the Commies, and everyone knew what one meant (pp.12–13).

Freddy's facile sneer, complacently automatic, is a long way from the Nazi purges, but, as Mrs Spark immediately reminds us by infusing sourer imagery into her bland prose, it has things in common with them: 'It was a diplomatic as well as a social error, here in this country. This was the first year of the Eichmann trial. Freddy felt like a wanted man who had been found hiding in a dark cupboard. He felt an urge to explain that he was not a mass-butcher and that he had never desired to become a *sturmbannführer, obersturmbannführer, superobersturmbannführer*' (p.13). The sequel to this, another nervy evening on the hotel terrace, is important, too. Mildly deploring intensity, Freddy finds himself fierily taken to task by a suddenly passionate Barbara elocuting the Apocalypse at him: 'I know of thy doings, and find thee neither cold nor hot; cold or hot, I would thou wert one or the other. Being what thou art, lukewarm, neither cold nor hot, thou wilt make me vomit thee out of my mouth' (p.16). And this stroke of civilized retaliation is not just in the book for the purpose of providing social comedy. Barbara's bruising quotation, later to be put to aggressive use by Freddy himself, calls attention to a fundamental part of Mrs Spark's thesis. Variously mocking intense commitment to a party or a group, the novel is far from deriding intensity itself. What it advocates is not a tepid caution, low-pressure existence, non-involvement, chary drawing-back from life. On the contrary, and with considerable eloquence, it urges involvement and concern, but channelled always towards the individual, not towards the clan.

This is brought out most clearly by the situation of Barbara Vaughan, at once very much concerned with an individual and, because of her hybrid heritage, difficult to place in any group. Faced with an Israeli guide who desires to know 'what category of person' (p.24) she is, she does obligingly attempt an outline of:

> The Golders Green Jewishness of her mother's relations and the rural Anglicanism of her father's, the Passover gatherings on the one hand and the bell-summoned Evensongs on the other, the talkative intellectuals of the one part and the kennel-keeping blood sportsmen of the other. . . . Barbara added that her parents themselves were, of course, exceptional, having broken away from their respective traditions to marry each other. And she herself was of course something else again (p.24).

But, as the man's continuing questions show his lack of understanding, she has to recognize that 'the essential thing about herself remained unspoken, uncategorized and unlocated' (p.24). A social and religious anthology, Barbara's identity is composed of very varied elements which cohere, however, into a harmony, so that she is 'all of a piece, a Gentile Jewess, a a private-judging Catholic, a shy adventuress' (p.173). And this means that she stands as a particularly clear example of Mrs Spark's contention that simple allegiance to a group or code must entail the suppression of some areas of personality. Significantly, the nearest she comes to giving loyalty to a single

institution and its creed is in her acceptance of the Catholic—
a word originally meaning 'universal'—faith. And even here,
besides being attracted to what she sees as the all-embracing
nature of this doctrine, its insistence on creation as a unity, its
rejection of division and separation, she retains her right of
free judgment and free action.

But, though Barbara herself resists social, racial, or religious
generalization, she is exposed, in the novel, to two main
dangers, both of which ironically stem from other people's
obsession with these things. A half-Jewish ancestry puts her at
very definite physical risk once she has entered Jordan; and
throughout the book she is psychologically menaced in a less
overt, but still troubling, way by the efforts of others to confine
her in some crudely conceived personality-type, seeing her not
as she is but as they would like her to be. Irritating but, on the
whole, comic in her relationship with Miles and Kathy, this
becomes more serious with regard to Ricky, the headmistress
with whom 'an unspoken agreement had been arrived at, to
the effect that they shared the same sense of humour and
disregard of men. It was, in a way, understood that when they
retired . . .' (p.43). At the opening of the novel, this assumption
that they are of the same kind and therefore somehow bound
together is already irksome:

> Once, after last summer's holidays when Barbara had fallen
> in love with Harry Clegg, Ricky was setting the senior girls
> an essay on the subject of the Second Coming to be illus-
> trated by scriptural texts; she demonstrated the procedure by
> quoting a passage on the return of Christ to judge the world:
> 'Then shall two be in the field; the one shall be taken and the
> other left. Watch therefore. . . .' Barbara, standing by,
> listened distantly to Ricky's moral implications, but heard
> closely the literal ones. It's certainly a point, thought
> Barbara, that two engaged in a common pursuit do not con-
> sequently share personal identity, and absurd though it is to
> affirm this evident fact, Ricky feels towards me as if the
> opposite were true. Sooner or later she'll have to find out
> that my destiny is different from hers (p.163).

As the book progresses, the pressure towards commitment
mounts; the relationship, with its false assumptions, becomes
another of the looming constrictions Barbara must fight against.

And she does fight, asserting her right to that scope and freedom necessary for the whole personality through some determined boundary-crossing. As a beginning, she attends the Eichmann trial, something she had earlier pigeon-holed away as 'apart from her purposes . . . political and temporary' (p.185). After this and its impact, she decides to take the risk of crossing to Jordan, unwilling to be penned in just one section of an entity. On the other side of the Mandelbaum Gate, she pushes through the barrier of overt respectability, fleeing the convent guest house with Freddy at dead of night as in comic represent-ation of her release from the imprisonment of type. Because of this, she eludes Ricky, who, true to her tendency to think in categories, is shown as hardening into an arch-bigot. And she resolves, again rejecting man-made separations, to marry Clegg even if the dictates of her church forbid it. Nor, it should be stressed, is this love-element a simple case of timely hetero-sexual rescue from crypto-Lesbian encroachment. Harry's involvement with Barbara is the opposite of Ricky's, but what makes it so is not that he is a man and she a woman: rather it is that one relationship is based on a deluded identification with kind, the other on an authentic perception of individuality:

> The form of their love seemed to her to derive from a faculty of inner knowledge which they both possessed, a passionate mutual insight so unique in her experience that she felt it to be unique in human experience. Harry Clegg—shock-haired, unhandsome—who would have guessed he would be her type? Miles referred to him as 'the red-brick genius'. But that was to reckon without Harry Clegg, who loved her. He loved her disguise as an English spinster not merely as dis-guise, but as part of her inexplicable identity. She was not an English spinster merely, but also a half-Jew, and was drawn to the equivalent quality in him that quite escaped both the unspoken definition 'Englishman of lower-class origin', and the spoken one 'red-brick genius' (p.38).

Barbara's faith, her belief that everything is integrated and therefore all division is temporary and meaningless, puts her intellectually on her guard against the dangers of group-narrowness, even if her mixed background did not already act as a safeguard against this. In the case of Freddy Hamilton, a sliding towards mild bigotry is generally corrected by his habitual fair-mindedness, 'an inward court of appeal with powers to reverse all varieties of mental verdicts' (p.127). Other qualities that make a personality inhospitable to the prejudiced or partisan are embodied in Abdul and Suzi Ramdez. Blue-eyed Arabs, products like Barbara of a non-conforming alliance, they stand as attractive figures of integrity. Both— 'brother and sister merged in a pact of personal anarchism' (p.99)—are open-minded, flexible, and independent. Both adroitly and mockingly avoid the pull of race, creed, sect. Like Freddy or Barbara, Abdul does on occasion derive comfort from association with a group, but, like theirs, his personal identity is always paramount. In a tuberculosis sanatorium, for instance: 'at night, when he lay among the rows of sleepers, he felt the security and comfort of being together with his own people. By day, he surged with individuality again' (p.103). To an extent, too, he thinks in category-terms, seeing a gulf between 'his generation as a whole' (p.82) and that Establishment he and his friends refer to as 'the System' (p.82). But, for the most part, Abdul appears as a free agent, mobile and receptive, his alertness always honed by what Mrs Spark presents as a crucial element in his character, something he acquired from an English girl he once had an affair with:

> self-humour. It was a form of endowment at the same time that it was a form of corruption. It undid him as a middle-class Arab enemy-hater with a career in the army or a position in business. . . . From the histrionic or dramatic point of view he was henceforth a spoiled Arab. He could not take any propaganda seriously. And she had unwittingly instilled scepticism into him, had taught him to be a doubter, and, at the same time, a faint-hearted hater (pp.98-9).

Salutary self-mockery of this kind, along with Abdul's cultivation of 'the knack of disinterestedness' (p.90)—'it was possible to do things for their own sake, not only possible but sometimes necessary for the affirmation of one's personal identity' (p.90)— ensures that he will not lapse into a mere group unit. It also, given the inflamed state of the Middle East, means he is driven underground, like other clandestine independents, when requiring satisfactorily untrammelled social life:

At Acre the people he had known were gone, but as happens, the place itself, by some invisible influence or tradition, had drawn the same sort of people, the young or the young at heart who belonged to nothing but themselves, for whose temperament no scope existed in any society open to them, and who by day enacted the requirements of their society. These were lapsed Jews, lapsed Arabs, lapsed citizens, runaway Englishmen, dancing prostitutes, international messes, failed painters, intellectuals, homosexuals. Some were silent, some voluble. Some were mentally ill, or would become so.

But others were not. Others were not, and never would become so; and would have been the flower and pride of the Middle East, given the sun and air of the mind, not yet to be available (p.104).

Through Abdul and Suzi—of whom it is said, 'Her strength lay in her vagueness about the limitations of her life; and her weakness derived from its actual limitations which she stood ready to demolish at any time' (p.224)—Mrs Spark is able to show the courage, flair, and pressure of living an emancipated life in an environment largely given over to sectarian strife, of a reliance on personal standards and motivation in a predominantly tribal atmosphere. They also, because of their marked physical similarity—Suzi 'with her very deep-blue eyes set in her brown face, looking extraordinarily like Abdul' (p.234)—enable her to illustrate the unimportance of another boundary: the sexual one. Initially attracted to Abdul, Freddy eventually—in that welling-up of confident vitality that follows his throwing-off of tepid constraints and conditioning—makes love to Suzi, who says: 'Freddy likes me, and I think it is because he likes Abdul. Never mind why, it's fine' (p.234).

Teasingly dissolving barriers in this way, the book itself also refuses to be restricted to one mode. Comedy and tragedy co-exist within it, linked by a common pattern. Ricky, questing for Barbara, farcically and unexpectedly finds an appropriate partner in Joe Ramdez: violence, when it finally occurs, happens horribly and unexpectedly not in war-ripped Palestine but—appropriately, it turns out—amidst the decorum of a Harrogate hotel. The comic and tragic are worked harmoniously into the same entity: and so are the religious and the secular. Barbara, 'a sexy pilgrim' (p.308), explains to Suzi: 'either religious faith penetrates everything in life or it doesn't. There are some experiences that seem to make nonsense of all separations of sacred from profane—they seem childish. Either the whole of life is unified under God or everything falls apart' (pp.307–8).

In *The Mandelbaum Gate*, the whole of the book is unified under the author and everything falls into place. Diverse as the novel's personnel and incidents may superficially appear, they have essential similarities: and are also drawn increasingly together by the narrowing spiral of the narrative. The Gardnors, for instance, are not just attached to the book by the fact that, living off the prejudice and dissensions of others, they represent anti-types of the disinterested and individuality-enhancing Abdul and Suzi: they are also worked into the novel's very tight intricacy of personal relationships—Rupert is Freddy's colleague: Ruth, it transpires, is a former acquaintance of Barbara; she is involved with Joe Ramdez and knows Suzi. Multiple link-ups of this kind are made with a great frequency. Barbara's attendant at Jericho turns out to be Ruth Gardnor; Ricky's informant about Barbara's marriage plans is Freddy's sister, barely mentioned Elsie; the priest who preaches in the Holy Sepulchre, angering its conservative custodians, is also the one with whose party Barbara crosses back through the Gate and who later, as he happens to be staying at her hotel, she consults about Harry's baptismal certificate. Plot liaison, helped on by coincidence, pulls people close. And cross-reference, too, wire-cutting its way through irrelevant division, works hard at achieving integration. The orthodox young Jews remind Freddy of his schooldays; the Israelis are reminiscent for Barbara of the Irish and the Welsh; excavations on Mount Tabor bring back memories of the previous summer—'even this small rectangle of archaeology related itself to her life. She recalled the dig at St. Albans' (p.35); an Arab boy watering the plants sends Freddy's mind back to young Hardcastle, the gardener's boy of his youth; Barbara is 'aware of various ways in which Ricky resembled Harry' (p.163); she scatters flower-seeds as Cousin Beryl did; Joanna is, in her bundle-bearing social work, like 'Freddy's aunts and sisters, all their school friends and the wives of Freddy's school friends' (p.136); Suzi can sympathize with Barbara's flight from Ricky—

similar situations arise in the harem; Freddy, using the word 'Victorian' triggers off in Barbara the memory-flash of a private family joke; Michael Aaronson, we are told, 'resembled Harry in his habit of making obvious rational comments about difficulties he did not feel were worth the trouble of analysing' (p.182): and so it goes on. Life, as here depicted, is composed of elements so inextricably connected as to make any attempt at division or dissociation manifestly absurd.

Not that there is anything homogeneous about the novel. On the contrary, it contains a very wide variety of character and scene; it ranges through a long and colourful gallery of life-styles, either compressed into sardonic miniature—'he had given Freddie an emancipated smile, then glanced at his wife before glancing at the clock; the Gardnors, in London, always had to go on somewhere else' (pp.242–3)—or set out more spaciously and lovingly, as in the two vignettes, from Barbara's girlhood, of life in the Thirties—Jewish at Golders Green, English County at Bells Sands—or the vividly informed sketches of Abdul's indigenous past and present. Much of the book's immediate appeal derives from Mrs Spark's ability to reproduce compellingly the salient externals of an ethos, her delight in capturing distinctive idiom, whether this be the tangled syntax of an old Jewish aunt—'Cucumbers! I have made yesterday cucumbers in pickle, twenty. Thirty-six last week in the jars I have with vinegar made, cucumbers' (p.34)—or the epistolary style of a middle-aged and mother-ridden diplomat:

> Then after dinner this evening we had some amusement from Joanna Cartwright's puppet theatre. (Do you recall, dearest Ma, that house at Lewes we used to visit, where they had some very grand puppets?—Joanna's puppets are not quite so grand.) She is extremely agile at managing their movements. There is also an extraordinary series of gramophone records which, by clever timing, accompany the puppets' movements perfectly. They seem to speak (pp.70–1).

But, gifted, like Freddy, with 'total perceptivity' (p.11), she also recognizes that these things are merely facets of the one entirety. Imaginative pressure forces the examples of diversity into agreement. Finally, for all its detailed catalogue of discord, the fiction is a model of that harmony so important to Mrs Spark aesthetically, metaphysically, and even ethically:

To Barbara, one of the first attractions of her religion's moral philosophy had been its recognition of the helpless complexity of motives that prompted an action, and its consequent emphasis on actual words, thoughts and deeds; the main thing was that motives should harmonize. Ricky did not understand harmony as an ideal in this sense. She assumed that it was both right that people should tear themselves to bits about their motives and possible for them to make up their minds what their motives were (pp.169–70).

Jerusalem, of course, is classically a microcosm, as Barbara at one point recalls:

> Jerusalem my happy home,
> When shall I come to thee?

> The lines sped to mind, and simultaneously seeing in her mind's eye the medieval text to which she was accustomed and, with her outward eye, an actual Gethsemane passively laid out on the Mount of Olives across the border, she sensed their figurative meaning piled upon the literal—'O my sweete home, Hierusalem'—and yearned for that magnetic field, Jerusalem, Old and New in one (pp.180–1).

Later, too, the priest in the Holy Sepulchre explains:

> there is a supernatural process going on under the surface and within the substance of all things. In the Jerusalem of history we see the type and shadow of that Jerusalem of Heaven that St. John of Patmos tells of in the Apocalypse. 'I, John', he says, 'saw in my vision that holy city which is the new Jerusalem, being sent down by God from Heaven, like a bride who has adorned herself to meet her husband.' This is the spiritual city that is involved eternally with the historical one (p.214).

In Mrs Spark's fiction, there is an artistic process going on under the surface, so that the historical city also becomes a symbolic one. Relevance sets up a magnetic field. Out of the novel's many instances of segregation a pattern of discord is created, a teeming emblem of barrier-building and the absurd futility of this. For this book, Mrs Spark has garnered an impressive multiplicity of interesting particulars. Equally impressively, these details, even the apparently trivial—like the present Ricky receives from an admirer: 'a bunch of roses, fourteen, each one of a different species' (pp.162–3)—are always finely tailored to the novel's theme. Talking about the book at the time of its publication, Mrs Spark said: 'I spent two months in Israel on "The Mandelbaum Gate". It took me a long time to write, two years. "The Prime of Miss Jean Brodie" took me eight weeks. "The Mandelbaum Gate" is much longer but it was also a great strain to write and I had to keep taking months off at a time. . . . It's a very important book for me, much more concrete and solidly rooted in a very detailed setting.'[16] And certainly, in its combination of large-scale documentary presentation and extremely insistent thematic relevance, *The Mandelbaum Gate* does represent the culmination of her phase of urban iconography. After it, the mythologizing of cities begins to wane: and, as she later came to think the novel structurally unbalanced—'It's out of proportion: the beginning is slow, the end is very rapid'[17]—Mrs Spark also goes back to working on a smaller canvas: 'I decided never again to write a long book. Keep them very short.'[18] And what appears on the canvas now is increasingly something that makes very 'unusual demands on the mind's eye'.[19]

5
Tense Present

In an extract from his *Sabbath Notebooks*, Nicholas Farringdon declared: 'There is a kind of truth in the popular idea of an anarchist as a wild man with a home-made bomb in his pocket. In modern times this bomb, fabricated in the back workshops of the imagination, can only take one effective form: Ridicule.'[1] Mrs Spark—influenced, she suggests, by having spent her formative years in Edinburgh: 'I imbibed, through no particular mentor, but just by breathing the informed air of the place, its haughty and remote anarchism'[2]—very much endorses this. 'Ridicule', she has stated categorically, 'is the only honorable weapon we have left':[3] and the speech from which this remark is taken, an address to the American Academy of Arts and Letters, goes on to urge at length and with some eloquence the paramount importance of satiric artistry. Characteristically entitled 'The Desegregation of Art', it really advocates two things: the abandonment of literature that, heavy with emotional appeal, aims at wringing pathos from depicted suffering, and the elevation in its place of the arts of satire and ridicule. What is wrong with the first, compassion-tugging form of writing, Mrs Spark feels, is that 'It cheats us into a sense of involvement with life and society but in reality it is a segregated activity.'[4] 'The art of protest', she complains, 'the art which condemns violence and suffering by pathetic depiction is becoming a cult separated from the actions of our life,'[5] for:

> what happens when, for example, the sympathies and the indignation of a modern audience are aroused by a play or a novel of the kind to which I have referred? I don't know for certain, but I suspect that a great number of the audience or of the readers feel that their moral responsibilities are sufficiently fulfilled by the emotions they have been induced to feel. A man may go to bed feeling less guilty after seeing such a play. He has undergone the experience of pity for the underdog. Salt tears have gone bowling down his cheeks. He has had a good dinner. He is absolved, he sleeps well. He

rises refreshed, more determined than ever to be the over-dog.'[6]

Skilled derision, on the other hand, is more trenchant in its effect:

> Solemn appeals to our sentiments of indignation and pity are likely to succeed only for the duration of the show, of the demonstration, or the prayer meeting, or the hours of reading. Then the mood passes, it goes to the four winds and love's labor's lost. But the art of ridicule, if it is on the mark—and if it is not true on the mark it is not art at all—can penetrate to the marrow. It can leave a salutary scar. It is unnerving. It can paralyze its object.'[7]

And this means that, defending literature of aggressive intent, she can go on to claim that: 'the only effective art of our particular time is the satirical, the harsh and witty, the ironic and derisive. Because we have come to a moment in history when we are surrounded on all sides and oppressed by the absurd.'[8] Glycerine soothes, but acid galvanizes. The art that temporarily inflames the tear-ducts, she insists, is inefficient, obliquely pandering to self-indulgence, and therefore thwarting its own purposes. What is now required is writing that more permanently stimulates the brain cells. And this will be achieved not simply by intensity of feeling but also—and more potently—by ingenuity of technique:

> I would like to see in all forms of art and letters, ranging from the most sophisticated and high achievements to the placards that the students carry about the street, a less impulsive generosity, a less indignant representation of social injustice, and a more deliberate cunning, a more derisive undermining of what is wrong. I would like to see less emotion and more intelligence in these efforts to impress our minds and hearts.'[9]

This is the rubric to which she now writes. The satiric element, always important in her fiction, is very much expanded: and the tone is necessarily harsher. Her narratives make their unwavering way through flagrant corruption; horror, a brief apparition in the earlier books, roams around more widely; the atmosphere is soured by violence of a particularly curdled kind—a hate-crazed husband who smashes his body to destruction in an attempt to sabotage his wife's career; a demented girl who lusts for violent death and hands her homicide the knife; slaughter amongst sex-glutted plutocrats, a triple-corpsed *crime passionel* nursed to red finale by the servants. And, handling gross evil of this kind, the novels move towards a style of mordant intricacy. Less room is given to character or narrative-expansion; the books are stringently pared down to steely essentials: but, at the same time, they become increasingly devious, stylized in such a way as to endow the type of story used—the fictional convention—with the significance previously attached to the physical setting. After *The Public Image*, these novels are, even by Mrs Spark's standards, very oblique: subtly, as well as fiercely, derisive.

But this process towards a new kind of artefact is a gradual one, and, in *The Public Image*, mainly manifests itself in a negative way. Drastically jettisoning inessentials in this work, Mrs Spark seems unsure what to do with the space she has created. Things are thrown out—not so much is made of the background as in the preceding books; less people are involved in the plot and it is comparatively straightforward; there is not such a rich garnering of comic particulars; the tone is less witty, the prose not so liable to crystallize into near-epigram, though from time to time it still does so: 'It was not customary to order children, however naughty, out of one's house, or call them beasts as if they were adults' (p.102);[10] 'What's good about not being bad?' (p.175)—but, technically, nothing really innovatory is added. 'An ethical shocker', Mrs Spark's dust-jacket summary of the novel, applies, in fact, more aptly to the next two books. Undeviatingly devoted to a single chain-reaction of hate, envy, and deception, *The Public Image* still has much in common with its predecessors, conforming, albeit rather skeletally, to the structural pattern they established. Time and place, though less effort is made to reproduce their distinctive character, are still important.

After London, Edinburgh, and Jerusalem, Mrs Spark, setting her novel's action in the mid-Sixties with their spurious cults of personality, their torrents of dubious publicity, turns to Rome: not the papal or imperial city, but the Rome of Via Veneto and *paparazzi*, film stars, scandal magazines, and ever-teetering fame. Against this gaudy backcloth, she examines a sombre theme: one owing its origin perhaps to that moment in the previous novel where Barbara Vaughan reflected wryly on the way 'her self-image was at variance with the image she presented to the world'.[11] In the case of Annabel Christopher, Mrs Spark's new protagonist, this gap, between insipid reality and that appetizing version of it served up, hot and spicy, in the gossip magazines, has become enormous. But, whereas Barbara, an intellectual and religious woman, hated seeming other than she was, Annabel is professionally dedicated to the preservation of an untrue image. She is a film star from Yorkshire, averagely untalented but with eyes that photograph dramatically. Discovered by an Italian producer, she has advanced towards the bright lights; helped on by his press secretary, a skilful weaver of publicity myths, she is now on the brink of international stardom. All depends, in the next few years, on the successful maintenance of her public image. And this needs care, since the legend assiduously assembled round Annabel and her husband has been one of 'a famous couple, impeccably formal by the light of day, voluptuously enamoured of each other under cover of night' (p.35): whereas, in reality, the much-vaunted and much-envied marriage is far from being a seductive idyll. The façade is posed and photographed:

> Francesca would . . . arrange . . . with a photographer to take a picture of Annabel lounging on the bed in her night-dress, one shoulder-band slipping down her arm and her hair falling over part of her face. Francesca disarranged the bed. She sat Frederick on the edge of the bed, in a Liberty dressing-gown, smoking, with a smile as of recent reminiscence. Or else Francesca had them photographed with a low table set with a lace-edged tray of afternoon tea, and the sun streaming in the window. Frederick held his cup and seemed to be stirring it gently and gravely while Annabel, sweet but unsmiling, touched the silver teapot with a gracious hand. 'We must get the two sides of your lives,' Francesca explained, in case there should be any doubt (pp.40–1).

But, behind it, things have been going wrong for years—drastically wrong: Mrs Spark has already, describing the couple's earlier days, quietly indicated bitter Frederick poring over Strindberg's *Dance of Death*.

An actor himself and a would-be writer, Annabel's husband

resents her successes, rather as Godfrey in *Memento Mori* envied Charmian her fame. His jealousy sometimes boils, but usually simmers for, though pained by the spectacle of Annabel's triumphs, he lacks courage to break away from the moneyed comforts they provide, and has even, when her image seemed precarious, complied to the extent of supplying her with a baby to sustain it. But as, with the passage of time, Annabel grows more successful, so Frederick grows more desperate: and, at last, sick of living a lie, he decides, with vicious logic, to die one. Using suicide, a crowd of disreputables, and a scattering of lying letters, he strikes savagely and after death at his wife's reputation. Shrewdly and ferociously, the publicity machine whirring and chattering around her all the while, Annabel battles back. By a near margin, she staves off disaster and preserves her image. Then, just as all seems secure, Billy O'Brien, a shabby hanger-on from drama school days, advances to the fore, attempting blackmail. In revulsion and irremediably, Annabel publicly shatters her image.

The gap between appearance and reality has always been important in Mrs Spark's fiction: she has always liked to trace the ways in which men deceive and self-deceive. In *The Public Image*, such mendacity swells into the outrageous and grotesque. In the world of this novel, there is falsity everywhere, falsity on a grand and elaborate scale. To begin with, the scene is Italy, where to posture is almost a natural response, where all subscribe with considerable enthusiasm to 'that principle of appearance appropriate to an occasion which they called *bella figura*' (p.111), and where there is a proverb that shruggingly declares, '*Se non è vero, è ben trovato*': 'If it isn't true, it's to the point' (p.43). This is innocent enough, but the old Roman streets afford instances of more sinister duplicity:

They drove round a deserted piazza with a fountain playing heartlessly, its bowl upheld by a group of young boys, which was built by the political assassin to placate his conscience; and past the palace of the cardinal who bore the sealed quiet of the whole within his guilt; with that girl now binding his body with her long hair for fun; while he lay planning, with a cold mind, the actions of the morning which were to conceal the night's evil: calumny, calumny, a messenger here and there, many messengers, bearing whispers and hints, and assured, plausible, eye-witness accusations. . . . Fixed inventions of deeds not done, accusations, the determined blackening of character (pp.92–3).

And these relics of deceit cast a grimly appropriate shadow over the events played out in front of them. Exaggeration and inventiveness, carried to the blatant and remunerative lengths required by Rome's film world, become dangerous and vicious, as natural responses are perverted or suppressed. Guile dominates. Truth is discarded, and, with it, all trace of moral standards. The marriage central to the book is an appalling travesty, a union held together by hate rather than love. Betrayal comes from the one person who should be reliable: a long friendship breeds not trust but treachery. Annabel is required to fight off lies with lies, publicly 'forgiving' the girl who has 'wronged' her, a pathetic figure with a drug-dulled brain; privately double-talking a deal with her husband's real mistress, herself tearfully anxious to maintain an image of respectability in the eyes of her family. Her sorrow is performed, not felt; the inquest staged like a scene for the cinema. All around her are packs of news-hungry journalists and cameramen, professional distorters of fact who can only be fended off by even greater distortion. In this milieu, when truth speaks, as it does through the mouth of a dumpy child—the doctor's daughter who, several times, undercuts Annabel's skilled attitudinizing—it is ordered out of the house.

Once again, a precept of Nicholas Farringdon is echoing behind Mrs Spark's intentions: 'Everyone should be persuaded to remember how far, and with what a pathetic thump, the world has fallen from grace.'[12] Once again, the symptoms of moral disease are damningly charted: lives spent in avid pursuit of trivia; neglect of truth and charity on an epidemic scale; lies told to others for profit and to the self for consolation. Yet here, amongst a most corrupt and spurious society, Mrs Spark moves, as in her two previous books, past diagnosis to cure.

In *The Girls of Slender Means*, Nicholas Farringdon was shown to be saved, ultimately, by a vision of evil; in *The Mandelbaum Gate*, Freddy Hamilton and Barbara Vaughan both experience regeneration through a kind of emotional late-flowering: and so it is with Annabel. During the novel, she undergoes a moral re-awakening, saved, ironically enough, by the baby she conceived in an attempt to save her image. We hear, early in the book, about her refusal to allow the child to be photographed, her reluctance to expose him to the artificial and meretricious world in which she lives. Increasingly, we are shown Annabel feeling lonely satisfaction in motherhood and a new longing for a freer life of loitering unnoticed and unphotographed. We see her, as her producer and O'Brien talk manoeuvres, gazing out through the open window at the stars. And, finally, the baby she has worked so hard to protect proves to have altered her, to have drawn her back towards natural and spontaneous life, towards truth. Despite the fact that there is no financial difficulty, Annabel refuses to pay O'Brien, refuses to endorse this last perversion and submit to blackmail from a detested familiar. She herself is unable to formulate her reasons for doing this, but Mrs Spark makes it quite clear that it is because she has grown in moral health. In one of his false suicide-notes, Frederick, with characteristic cliché, had referred to Annabel as 'a beautiful shell, like something washed up on the sea-shore, a collector's item, perfectly formed, a pearly shell—but empty, devoid of the life it once held' (p.141); finally, as the mother stands unnoticed with her baby in the sunshine, waiting for a plane to Greece, Mrs Spark returns deliberately to this image, and, in a finely effective stroke, infuses it—as Annabel herself has now been infused—with a new vitality: 'She was as pale as a shell. She did not wear her dark glasses. Nobody recognised her as she stood, having moved the baby to rest on her hip, conscious also of the baby in a sense weightlessly and perpetually within her, as an empty shell contains, by its very structure, the echo and harking image of former and former seas' (p.192).

Annabel, of course, who is 'unaccustomed to organise anything' (p.8), unreflective, and 'had never been given to problems' (p.55), is rather different from the usual Spark protagonist. Generally, the central figures of these novels are highly literate, intellectual, and religious, gifted and afflicted with insight, articulate and penetrating. Annabel is none of these things. She has no religion and works at a much lower level of awareness, her intelligence directed not towards the scrutiny of others but the simple preservation of herself and her child. It is a major triumph of this book that, working within the restrictions of this girl's character, Mrs Spark is able to depict an authentic moral growth.

There is austerity in the rest of the novel, too, large effects being achieved by characteristically slender means. Even the orgy—a word set echoing sardonically through the pages of this book, much as 'ignorant', 'immoral', 'bachelor', or 'prime' were played up and down the scales in earlier works—is presented with a bleak restraint, the essentially unglamorous nature of debauch emerging in the few stark details Mrs Spark briefly and unemotionally highlights—a smiling man, for instance: 'the man continued smiling; it was a smile with the mouth only, and she saw him move a hand to his mouth to try to stop the smile and to readjust the facial muscles; she realised then that the man was rather ill. She looked round to see how many others had come fresh from drug feast' (p.71).

At the centre of the two preceding novels lay a momentary glimpse of hell, one spot where the prevailing moral greyness became totally black. In *The Girls of Slender Means*, this was Selina, pushing her way through friends in mortal danger to rescue a dress; in *The Mandelbaum Gate*, Eichmann in his glass cell. In *The Public Image*, the tableau of evil is a scene where Annabel, checking on her baby's safety during the party, finds that even this retreat has been tainted:

A street lamp cast a dim night-light into the room, and now she saw that someone had been in there. There was a brandy-bottle lying on the floor between the baby and a chest-of-drawers. Annabel smelt it. It smelt only of brandy. But she was frightened now, lest some drug-addict should slip in to the room and perhaps harm the baby in her absence. She lay down on the narrow bed for about ten minutes, letting the noises of the night break over her' (pp.77–8).

This juxtaposition of the healthy and the stale, the natural and the artificial, a baby and a brandy bottle, creates a strong and sinister impact. Here, as elsewhere, Mrs Spark's ingredients are sparse, yet the effect achieved is far from one of poverty. The reader is reminded of one of the observations of Luigi Leopardi, Annabel's director, as he watches her scheme to save her image: 'Her talent . . . is a rich one. As in life . . . it is the very rich who understand thrift while the poor spend quickly on trifles' (pp.144).

Yet, although Mrs Spark is unflinching in her insistence on the evil behind the good life, the bitterness behind the *dolce vita*, *The Public Image*, like all her fiction, is very far from depressing: for, even as the moralist is indicating waste and futility, the craftsman—no stranger, after all, to the manufacturing of plausible deception—is paying amused tribute to the ingenuity exercised in creating and sustaining the lies of publicity. Mrs Spark is not a writer to overrate intelligence— unguided by morality, it is useless, she insists: and Annabel, for all her professional dexterity, is shown quite plainly to be destroying herself—but she is not the person to underrate it either. The devil is mockingly given his due. There is relish as well as condemnation in the pinning-down of insincerities, the artist in the author revelling, even as the moralist winces, at the enormities perpetrated with such blind flair and confidence: 'Annabel did not forget to look up at the hospital windows; sure enough, most of them were occupied by peering and bobbing heads. She placed her sad smile up there, too' (pp. 159–60).

'I love the glossies and the newspapers and film mags,' Mrs Spark has said, 'and that's where I find a lot of my material'.[13] In *The Public Image*, this interest shows itself in several ways. The novel concentrates upon a sector of society particularly dear to disclosure-journals; it deals with a campaign to keep their intrusions at bay; and it pays wry tribute to the lurid vitality of these publications:

> these sunny glossies of Italy beamingly scandalised the just and the unjust alike, churning up the splendour of their wickedness, weekly. The range of emotions was as grand as Grand Opera, but no subtler. A clandestine child, preferably a son, of a film star is dicovered; or an opera singer tells of the persecution she currently endures at the hands of the tenor's wife (under the headline 'Assunta is Jealous of Me'); divorce in a royal family is a standard thriller, or any story involving mother-love, especially when the theme turns on the sacrifice of a steady lover. Sheer villains, utter innocents— the world's most complicated celebrities have been cast anew in these simple roles (pp.35–6).

Mrs Spark's material is deliberately similar. Her story, too, is a chronicle of jealousy, hate, violence and infidelity: her fuliginous exposé is relieved by the light of mother-love, that of a famous film star for her son. Where there is a difference, of course, is in Mrs Spark's style of writing. Her subject may be scandal, but her prose is chaste. And this contrast becomes a powerful satiric weapon. There are no open denunciations in this fiction, no overt moral analyses or propaganda: but a bizarre counterpoint of style and content ensures that there is final condemnation. The quiet accuracy of the prose acts as damning foil to the strident falsity depicted; the precise immaculacies of the diction tacitly deride the sprawling squalors they retail; publicity's windy myths, mockingly inflated, phrase by phrase, are punctured and brought sagging down to earth by contemptuous colloquialism: 'Within a few weeks, throughout Italy and beyond, it was decidedly understood, thoroughly suggested, hinted and memorised, that in private, inaccessible to all possible survey, and particularly in bed, Annabel Christopher, the new star who played the passionate English governess, let rip' (p.42). The rightness of the language provides sufficient commentary upon the wrongness of the content. And in her next book, *The Driver's Seat* (1970), Mrs Spark continues this technique, besides introducing several other interesting ones.

In this work, she carefully sets her plot against environmental anonymity, some of it occurring in transit—airport departure and arrival lounges, hotels, bars, department stores—most of it in what seems, but is never said, to be the Italy of mass vacation, tourist crowds, and halting, polyglot communication. Where the story happens is not specified: when it does is very definite. Contemporary as the traffic-anarchy to which it makes such reference, *The Driver's Seat* is very much a parable of nowadays. In a piece narrated—for the first time, for her—in the present tense, Mrs Spark turns her attention to the tense present.

The story deals with Lise, unpartnered, in her thirties, heading south from Denmark for a holiday and, she hopes, a meeting with a man who is her 'type' (p.51).[14] The situation sounds familiar, but rapidly this cliché of the novelette—single girl on expectant holiday—is twisted into savage parody. The man Lise dresses to attract and roams the streets to find is not a lover but a murderer. Death is the consummation that she wants. This is the novel's central travesty, but others cluster round it, the world of *The Driver's Seat* being one where, constantly, the normal is reversed, the usual distorted: a world in which the female hunts the male, the victim her murderer, eagerly and leaving clues behind her as she does so. What the novel is concerned with is the way contemporary society militates against the natural. And so, with typical appropriateness, Mrs Spark takes and then deforms conventional material: the abnormality with which her novel deals is mirrored in its very story-line.

It is an apt device and characteristic of the artistry that makes this fiction so remarkable. Brief yet complex, *The Driver's Seat* is a product of great formal discipline, each part being carefully related to the novel's theme and necessary to the structure of the whole, its threads of imagery weaving together to display the fabric of contemporary life: a fabric, they insist—which like the one that Lise rejects with horror in the book's first scene— is utterly synthetic and unnatural.

And the unnatural, in fact, pervades the book, from its opening line—' "And the material doesn't stain." the salesgirl says' (p.9)—to its bizarre conclusion, where psychotic Lise literally and metaphorically drives a sexual maniac to kill her. There is, for instance, the marked emphasis on wrapping and protection. Trivial in isolation, references to this recur throughout the work and, cumulatively, have their effect. Clothes, food, implements, documents: continually, almost obsessively, attention is drawn to the way that these are covered up by plastic or by paper,[15] and, finally, in the last moments of the book, the reason for this emphasis on 'wrapped-up objects of different shape' (p.121) emerges very clearly. Hopelessly, Lise's murderer attempts escape and, as he does, 'sees already the gleaming buttons of the policemen's uniforms, hears the cold and the confiding, the hot and the barking voices, sees already the holsters and epaulets and all those trappings designed to protect them from the indecent exposure of fear and pity, pity and fear' (p.160). This is a civilization, the recurrent motif of covering suggests, in which the natural is held at one remove, the real thing—even when this is genuine emotional response— kept behind some outer layer that protects it or conceals. And because of this, there is a constant stress upon externals: something which can be mindless—like the woman from

Johannesburg Lise encounters at an airport stall, looking for books that are 'predominantly pink or green or beige' (p.30) to match the decor of her bedrooms—or vicious—as when a hippy is ejected from a store because he does not look respectable because his garb offends convention.

Lise, too, to register her protest and her abnormality, relies upon appearance. The novel opens with her buying clothes: and, having chosen them, a clashing, garish mixture, she informs the astounded salesgirl, 'Those colours of the dress and the coat are absolutely right for me. Very natural colours' (pp.15–6). There is irony here, of course—the 'lurid outfit' (p.27) really is right for Lise's lurid psychology: its discordancy is a natural match for hers—just as there is, later, irony, when a woman mocks her with the words, 'Dressed for the carnival!' (p.101). In the deadliest sense, she is indeed dressed for the carnival, for the farewell to flesh, her clothes and the gaudy paperback she flaunts designed in part, at least, as desperate signalling to the man who will destroy her.

Why Lise desires this violent extinction, why she is running towards the knife, is established quickly in the novel's opening scenes, where she is shown, first, reacting with hysterical revulsion to the information that the dress she wears is made from new synthetic fibre, doesn't stain; then, at the tedious heart of the accountant's office where she works—'she has five girls under her, and two men. Over her are two women and five men' (p.12); and, finally, inside her home, a flat described —with sardonic suitability—in prose that is kept functional and colourless until, at the very last, it is allowed to break into a wistful damning image of the natural beauty and vitality that are so lacking here:

> the furniture is all fixed, adaptable to various uses, and stackable. Stacked into a panel are six folding chairs, should the tenant decide to entertain six for dinner. The writing desk extends to a dining table, and when the desk is not in use it, too, disappears into the pinewood wall, its bracket-lamp hingeing outward and upward to form a wall-lamp. The bed is by day a narrow seat with overhanging bookcases; by night it swivels out to accommodate the sleeper. . . . A small pantry-kitchen adjoins this room. Here, too, everything is contrived to fold away into the dignity of unvarnished

pinewood. . . . The swaying tall pines among the litter of cones on the forest floor have been subdued into silence and into obedient bulks (pp.19–20).

This—'Nowhere special' (p.80), as she says—is the starting point of Lise's odyssey, but travel—her obsessive search for what she calls 'the lack of an absence' (p.105)—brings little alteration. The impersonality and the sterility from which she starts accompany her on her journey and are waiting at the other end to greet her, for *The Driver's Seat* is contemporary, too, in being a story of the global village, of a world infected with a deadly, artificial sameness. This is an environment devoid of the vitality of difference. The same goods are on sale at the northern airport from which Lise departs as at the city in the south where she arrives. The nationalities mix aimlessly together. Conversations take place in the basics of four languages against a neutral background. Travel, in this world, appears pointless but, ironically, has swelled to frightening proportions. Bill, the macrobiotic food enthusiast whose fumbling sexual chase of Lise counterpoints her desperate hunt, intends, he says, to give a lecture called 'The World—Where Is It Going?' (p.136). And this could stand, most fittingly, as a subtitle to the novel, filled, as it is, with references to movement and *en masse*: 'July thousands' (p.29) milling round the airport, streams of traffic, mobs of tourists, even a stampede.[16]

It is, however, as the chosen name, *The Driver's Seat*, suggests, the car that gives this book its central symbol: an effective one, bringing together, as it does, the two ideas of mass movement and the shielding of the natural behind an artificial shell. Implicitly, in fact, the car comes, in this work, to stand as an equivalent for modern urban man: a standardized exterior, a tough casing round the vulnerable and human, steered by the mind, the seat of judgment and control, the driver's seat. The streams of cars along the roads rhyme grimly with the crowds mechanically proceeding on the pavements. 'I'm afraid of traffic,' Lise significantly says. 'You never know what crackpot's going to be at the wheel of another car' (p.82). Her story is the story of just such a situation—loss of control, a self-destructive drive—in a society where people pass each other as insentiently as traffic.

'You become what you eat,' (pp. 50, 55) it is emphasized:

and, throughout the book, there is the implication that, nourished by the unnatural, men have become unnatural; reliant on machinery, come to resemble machines. In this setting, Lise's raw reality is not merely an anomaly: it also represents a threat, leads to 'inquietude and fear . . . secret dismay' (p.156). 'Why is everybody afraid of me?' (p.56) she asks, the answer being that her strident, maimed humanity pulls disturbingly at feelings those around her want to stifle. Her behaviour dangerously challenges the whole tacit conspiracy which acts as basis to this life of surface and machines: and so her efforts to provoke attention meet only with hostility —often taking the form of jeering laughter, another instance of the warping of the natural—or glazed oblivion. Despite the titles which they proudly boast—he is, 'an Enlightenment Leader' (p.55) and she 'a Witness' (p.91)—both of those Lise spends most time with, Bill and Mrs Fiedke, remain quite blind to her real nature. Both see her in the way most convenient for them. And both, it is noticeable, invariably trade in hefty simplification: he categorizing everything as either Yin or Yang, the female or male principle; she lamenting the difference between 'These days' (p.82) and '*those* days' (p.78). If emphasis on covering leads to locking of the natural behind the artificial, so, it is suggested, this life of movement in increasing numbers—' "It's getting late," says Lise. "There are so many faces. Where did all the faces come from?" ' (p.108)—brings about submergence of the individual in the mass: this, in its turn, encourages a dangerous tendency to generalize. Established national and, much to Mrs Fiedke's maundering dismay, sexual boundaries seem, in this novel, to be breaking down, but they are being fast replaced by other barriers. In a world of international mingling, fresh blocs coagulate and oppose: young and old, hip and conventional, students and police.

Asked in interview about the novel, Mrs Spark has said, 'It's a study, in a way, of self-destruction'.[17] This is true, though in the widest sense; the self-destructive urge in Lise presented both as mirror and as symptom of that all around her, her madness but one instance of a general malaise. It is not merely on the level of a twisted shocker—crazed victim engineering her own slaughter—that *The Driver's Seat* is troubling. Progressing through grey scenes of automated, overcrowded limbo, past surreal tableaux of derangement, to the culmination of a woman screaming, in four languages, for death, it is by far the darkest book that Mrs Spark has yet produced. And the darkness is achieved, to some extent, by a reversal of what, in the immediately preceding works, was her usual procedure. In each of these three books, *The Girls of Slender Means*, *The Mandelbaum Gate*, and *The Public Image*, there was, at some point in the narrative, a scene of utter evil and absurdity. In *The Driver's Seat* the opposite technique is used. Now criminal absurdity is let loose through the book and there is only one glint in the darkness, a moment when Lise's potential, a potential warped by the unnatural life she is compelled to lead, is briefly spotlit:

> 'It was very kind of you to come along with me,' says Mrs. Fiedke, 'as it's so confusing in a strange place. Very kind indeed.'
> 'Why shouldn't I be kind?' Lise says, smiling at her with a sudden gentleness (p.81).

Like the graceful old Pavilion—now converted into a restaurant —where she dies, or the ruins she and Mrs Fiedke go to visit— relics of a different way of life almost submerged now in the chaos of the modern city—this fragment of natural humanity survives amidst the diseased urgencies of her psychosis.

But, if the normal is allowed its moment, it is to the abnormal that the book is mainly given up. And to create the unnerving atmosphere appropriate to this, Mrs Spark employs a number of devices. Central to the novel and most obvious is her use of parody—parody of the thriller and the magazine-romance— reinforced by numerous inversions and distortions. Traditional attributes of female and male—the Yin and Yang of Bill's macrobiotic theories—sufferer and agent, victim and murderer blur weirdly together, most notably, of course, in Lise, with whom, too, tears and laughter, frequently referred to, mingle oddly, run into each other: the general ambience being of such dislocation that lines such as Bill's wry plaint, 'I'm queer for girls' (p.137), or Mrs Fiedke's 'Look at the noise' (p.82) seem perfectly in keeping. And, furthering this sense of travesty, Lise's activities seem, at times, to parody those of the novelist, not just in her manipulation of the characters around her, but in her habit of collecting facts and re-arranging these into a false but useful pattern, quite different from that already seen. 'I got mixed up in a student demonstration', she says to Bill surreally scrambling the events of her day, 'and I'm still crying from the effect of tear-gas. I had a date at the Hilton for dinner with a very important Sheik but I was too late, as I went to buy him a pair of slippers for a present. He'd gone on safari. So he wasn't my type, anyway. Shooting animals' (pp.135-6). Like a distorting-mirror image, the fictitious is set inside the fictional.

All these twists, the parodies and the inversions, point insistently towards the book's concern with abnormality: as do the lunatic-fringe theories advanced by Bill and Mrs Fiedke, and the various cameos of senselessness that flicker past from time to time—a girl frenetically continuing her dance after the music has stopped; a riot suddenly raging down a city street; a dream-like parade of Arabs, the entourage of some Near-Eastern Sheik on the move after a military coup. And there is, too, a sick man near Lise on her plane and said to look 'some sort of mental distance from reality' (p.52), a phrase applicable to most of the characters in this book, characters who, it is further noticeable, are also at some mental distance from each other. Like Mrs Spark's first fictional work, *The Comforters*, this novel frequently returns to the idea of people held apart by non-communication, shows again constant, almost frantic, social interaction without any corresponding comprehension.

Technically, however, *The Driver's Seat* is very different from that earlier book. Writing this novel, constructing her 'why-dunnit' (p.151), Mrs Spark has placed upon her talent rigorous restrictions, has limited herself to a purely external view of her protagonist and her prose to a present tense that generates a nervy, urgent atmosphere. In addition, and aptly enough in a work concerned with contemporary absurdity, *The Driver's Seat* owes some of its techniques to Robbe-Grillet and the anti-novelists. In *The Mandelbaum Gate*, musing on such writers, Barbara Vaughan mentally characterized their productions as 'repetition, boredom, despair, going nowhere for nothing, all of which conditions are enclosed in a tight, unbreakable statement of the times at hand'[18]—an observation that provides an accurate summary of *The Driver's Seat*. As in the *nouveau roman*, there is here constant and meticulous description, repeated cataloguing of external detail, 'the drama of exact statement':[19] though Mrs Spark differs drastically from her models—first, in obviously regarding their procedure as sufficiently eccentric to find its ideal use in a work concerned with derangement, and, secondly, in that, while implications from the data presented are not overtly taken up in the novel, they are intended to be noted. Here, as in all Mrs Spark's books, the various elements are held in the firm grip of parable: there is no slack. Everything is made to earn its keep. Details, no matter how trivial they may seem, are pencilled in because they have significance. In a department store, for instance, Lise wanders, at one stage, past some television sets on which are seen 'a charging herd of buffalo, large on one screen and small on the other' (p.94). It is only a brief glimpse, but, unobtrusively, the picture falls into place in a chain of imagery, one of several references all carrying an oblique reminder of the animal needs and instincts still very much at play in modern, mechanized society: references to 'unencumbered youth who swing and thread through the crowds like antelopes' (p.79), to 'the waiting herd' (p.80) at a traffic crossing, to Lise seen as 'a stag scenting the breeze' (p.107), to mindless large-scale motion—'Suddenly round the corner comes a stampede' (p.109). Concentrated as it is, the novel calls for concentration: words and phrases—'the time of my life' (p.13), 'circus' (p.23), 'psychedelic' (p.46), 'macrobiotic' (p.48), 'carnival' (p.101)—taking on connotations beyond the casual, demotic usage, innocent-sounding chatter wrapping itself round serious hints—'if Mr. Fiedke was alive today he would be a Witness too. In fact he was one in many ways without knowing it', complacently announces Mrs Fiedke, herself just such an unsuspecting witness.

In this novel, Mrs Spark, it seems, has decided to destroy not just her protagonist but, once and for all, her own false reputation as a comic and therefore, it has too often been assumed, not very serious writer. *The Driver's Seat* has its moments of humour, usually in scenes where the lack of mutual understanding that pervades the book reaches some particularly farcical impasse, as in the early episode where a bewildered salesgirl eagerly presses stain-resistant wares on outraged Lise:

'Doesn't stain?'
The customer has flung the dress aside.
The salesgirl shouts, as if to assist her explanation. 'Specially treated fabric. . . . If you spill like a drop of

sherry you just wipe it off. Look, Miss, you're tearing the neck.'

'Do you think I spill things on my clothes?' the customer shrieks. 'Do I look as if I don't eat properly?' (p.11).

This loud encounter, building to crescendo—'flung', 'shouts', 'shrieks'—between irrational fury and incomprehension is, in its black way, amusing, but it is also relevant, carefully related to the book's concerns. There are, in *The Driver's Seat*, no jokes for their own sake.

The work is always disciplined, taut, and beautifully structured. The form displays those qualities—order, purpose, harmony, control—ominously submerged in the society depicted: and this, along with the precise and subtle prose, ensures that, for all the grimness of its bulletins—sick authenticity against an inauthentic world—the book is finally invigorating. From a formal point of view, of course, the most interesting and innovatory aspect of this work is the way in which the novel's mode is sardonically made to match its matter. Two literary genres, both of a fairly lowly kind, the sort of thing that people read when travelling, like Lise, or on holiday—the thriller and the girl-finds-boy romance—are twined together, their standard features being strategically deranged and warped to accommodate a warped, deranged protagonist. An earlier claim of Mrs Spark—'the theme that one is writing about dictates its own form'[20]—takes on new, intensified significance, with *The Driver's Seat*: and very much retains it, too, with her next book, *Not to Disturb* (1971).

The literary modes deployed, this time, are Gothic horror and Jacobean tragedy. The locale is that of melodrama, as premonitions at the lodge, gore in the library, and frenzy in the attic rapidly establish. Night thickens, as fog rises from the lake, round a sequestered mansion where baron, baroness, and secretary-lover, lethally entangled, rage their way to multiple destruction. The erotic playmates' fatal tantrums are somewhat obscured, however, by the swelling din elsewhere. This is a very noisy book. Upstairs, a cretin-heir howls and hurls crockery; outside, indignant fists pound on the door, while gale-slammed shutters crack like pistol-shots: for it is, of course, a stormy night. Nature herself is out in sympathy, as the convention insists, entering into the spirit of the thing with meteorological panache. Around the shambles in the chateau, thunder, lightning, high winds, and torrential rain generate a necessary climate of catastrophe. There is a great deal of mock-Gothic orchestration—'a sound like a human bark followed by an owl-screech. Anne the masseuse adds a further cry to the night' (p.53),[21] 'a double crash of thunder beats the sky above the roof. A long wail comes from the top of the house' (p.100). Even the internal telephone—'a bronchial and aged raven, penetrating the room' (p.75)—does its gruesome bit: 'the instrument wheezes' (p.26), 'it hisses back through its windpipe' (p.99), 'gives a brief gusty sigh' (p.100). Other customary props of *grand guignol* subliminally lurk in imagery— the doomed trio 'haunt the house . . . like insubstantial bodies, while still alive' (p.37)—or in implicit comparison—a vampiric crew of servants metaphorically battening upon the blood of others. Yet the plot, for all its play with these flesh-creeper stereotypes—carnage at the mansion, screams in the night, patrician depravities ending in a welter of blue-bloodshed—is not, as such fictions tend to be, an arbitrary accumulation of disasters.

Earned inevitability, as the servants recognize, is governing the action. The abattoir behind the library doors is a foredoomed conclusion: and appropriate trappings from another genre are festooned throughout the narrative to remind of this. The Gothic shocker with its sprawling sensations is not, after all, the only art-form that traditionally chronicles erring aristo- cracy's violent extinction. The fall of those of high degree, amidst louche circumstance, vice breeding spectacular cal- amity, is the usual framework, too, for Jacobean tragedy. And there are here, of course, many similarities to this. There is a background of febrile, nerve-fed sexuality. Classic ingredients— ambition, treachery, jealousy, and madness—are stirred into the brew. Omens and dreams and ironies dutifully congregate. And as the high-born sinners progress, self-impelled, towards catastrophe, servants keep up a moralizing commentary. The first words spoken in the novel come from the usefully literary butler and immediately place the fiction's whereabouts: ' "Their life," says Lister, "a general mist of error. Their death, a hideous storm of terror."—I quote from *The Duchess of Malfi* by John Webster, an English dramatist of old' (p.5).

And, throughout the night, from time to time, he pins further borrowed captions to the tragedy: murmurs *'Sic transit gloria mundi'* (p.25), as the opulent protagonists assemble for the kill; recites, in the vast Klopstock drawing-room:

> Think in this battered Caravanserai
> Whose doorways are alternate Night and Day,
> How Sultan after Sultan with his Pomp
> Abode his Hour or two, and went his way (p.47);

and, to the milling, post-mortem press, dispenses Shirley's rhetorical commonplaces:

> The glories . . . of our blood and state
> Are shadows, not substantial things;
> There is no armour against fate;
> Death lays his icy hand on kings:
> Sceptre and crown
> Must tumble down,
> And in the dust be equal made
> With the poor crooked scythe and spade (p.154).

Like its classic prototypes, *Not to Disturb* is organized into five acts; its narrative technique—all characters externally presented, only their actions and their speech recorded—brings it close to a transcript of something occurring on a stage; and there are some resounding curtain-lines: ' "Let's proceed," he says, leading the way to the servants' quarters. "There remain a good many things to be accomplished and still more chaos effectively to organize" ' (p.72). The Unities, too, are stringently respected. The novel is restricted in place to the big house outside Geneva. Its time-span is confined to a single night, while several references further insist that, in any case, time itself is a unity, that 'the whole of eternity is present "now" ',[22] as Mrs Spark wrote in her Proust essay. 'Let us not split hairs . . . between the past, present and future tenses' (p.6), says Lister, speaking also of 'what is to come, or has already come, according as one's philosophy is temporal or eternal' (p.17): and his waving away of 'vulgar chronology' (p.66) is helped on by the instance of a phone call from America: 'They should have telephoned yesterday. But it's still yesterday over there. They always ring in the middle of the night from the United States of America. They think that because they are five hours back we also are five hours back' (pp.102–3). Mainly, though, he is pointing to the notion that the victims' ends are in their corrupt beginnings, that 'what's done is about to be done and the future has come to pass' (p.12). What is happening, he insists, has the unity of chain-reaction. 'There is a vast difference', it is remarked, 'between events that arise from and those that merely follow after each other. Those that arise are preferable' (p.111). And *Not to Disturb* has, very markedly, this streamlined necessity. 'How like the death wish is to the life-urge! How urgently does an overwhelming obsession with life lead to suicide!' (p.19) says Lister, going on to add of those caught up in this: 'Sex is not to be mentioned. . . . To do so would be to belittle their activities. On their sphere sex is nothing but an overdose of life. They will die of it, or rather, to all intents and purposes, have died. We treat of spontaneous combustion' (p.19). There is a constant stress on the inevitability of the event-sequence: 'To put it squarely . . . the eternal triangle has come full circle' (p.39), 'let nature take its course' (p.53), 'What is to emerge must emerge' (p.72), 'Only remember that nothing peculiar has been going on, as indeed it hasn't' (p.141). As more or less the impresario of the tragedy—'Group yourselves apprehensively' (p.146), he tells the other servants as the press arrive—it is Lister's task to keep contingency at bay, shutting the gates to the outer world, ensuring that the build-up in the library is not disturbed, and censoring irrelevance: 'This is not the time for inconsequential talk' (p.5). Schooled in the tragic conventions, he is, of course, aware—'one foresees the unforeseen' (p.109)—that on such occasions it is usual for the unexpected to accompany the inevitable on its syllogistic progress. And, confident of this— 'There was sure to be something unexpected' (p.12)—he easily retrieves the break-away narrative of the Klopstock inheritance, plaiting it deftly into the main course of events by a timely marriage, at which the bride wears a coat belonging to one of the violently deceased and carries, as bouquet, part of the funeral wreath intended for the others.

Further threats to the unity of action—sporadic sorties into the narrative by Anne, the masseuse, and Alex, her transvestite accomplice—are, at first, dismissed by Lister as quite negligible: 'They don't come into the story' (p.51). In the next paragraph, however, they do, and continue to hover stubbornly around the Klopstock mansion until the author herself takes a hand:

> Meanwhile the lightning, which strikes the clump of elms so that the two friends huddled there are killed instantly without pain, zig-zags across the lawns, illuminating the lily pond and the sunken rose garden like a self-stricken flash photographer, and like a zip-fastener ripped from its garment by a sexual maniac, it is flung slap-dash across Lake Leman and back to skim the rooftops of the house, leaving intact, however, the well-insulated telephone wires which Lister, on the telephone to Geneva, has rather feared might break down (pp.143–4).

Mockingly, the syntax insists on the irrelevance of these interlopers. They are not even the subject of the sentence that contains their death, but dispatched in a very subordinate clause. The lightning, menacing the necessary telephone wires, has priority. Even the imagery used of it possesses more pertinence than hopelessly contingent Anne and Alex: there are flash-photographers and a zip-ripping maniac in the central narrative as well as in the similes, and the aptness is jokingly pulled tighter still by a subsequent announcement that 'The Swiss invented the zip-fastener' (p.153).

All this is, of course, highly and deliberately artificial: for, in *Not to Disturb*, what Mrs Spark is setting out to do is to put together a simulated Gothic horror tale and a simulated tragedy. Traditionally associated with high life, the genres she rifles for her cerebral pastiche are well suited to the novel's aristocratic content: but much more important is the fact that what is offered here is counterfeit, not the genuine thing. Simulation is, in fact, the subject of this book as well as the technique employed for it. Synthetic horror and synthetic tragedy are the appropriate modes for an account of what have been very synthetic lives. The Klopstock milieu is one of masquerade. Their house, for instance, is a counterfeit, an eleven-year-old compound of imported antiquities—Regency banisters, Adam mantelpieces, and a parquet floor that, as Lister explains:

> once belonged to a foreign king. He had to flee his throne. He took the parquet of his palace with him, also the door-knobs. Royalty always do, when they have to leave. They

take everything, like stage-companies who need their props. With royalty, of course, it all is largely a matter of stage production. And lighting. Royalty are very careful about their setting and their lighting. As is the Pope. The Baron resembled royalty and the Pope in that respect at least. Parquet flooring and door-handles. The Baron bought them all in a lot with the house, when the old king passed away (pp.45–6).

Amidst a decor of expensive camouflage—'*trompe-l'oeil* chequered paving' (p.14), 'A porcelain snow-white lamb, artfully woolly' (p.42), parquet layers that conceal 'planks of dusty common wood' (p.44)—these people are habituated to routines of self-gratifying artificiality, fatally devoid of honesty and spontaneity. The Baroness, going through a gracious rigmarole of spurious charm in the warmth of her car, while Theo, a captive audience, shivers in the icy wind outside, shows one kind of egocentric pretence: the falsity of the performance being further underscored by its immediate sequel where she reveals her intention of dismissing him or, rather, using a stand-in for what would be a less agreeable scene to perform, delicately delegates someone else to do this for her: 'Arrange something to make it easy, Lister. The Baron and I would be so grateful' (p.36). Most relevant to the catastrophe, however, are the sexual charades the Klopstocks have a taste for, pornographic scenarios fleshed out by an affluence-procured cast of servants, secretaries, and cousins. Providing blackmail-material in the form of films and tape-recordings, these partly contribute to the final bloodshed in an obvious way. More important, though, is the suggestion that these fantasies and simulations, used to introduce a bit of edge into a flaccid world, have taken on a merciless momentum of their own. Playing at erotic situation-games, the Klopstocks are ultimately trapped inside one. The fictional stereotypes they have perversely toyed with close in vengefully around them. Having attempted to treat the natural as artefact, subject to pattern and necessity, they find themselves hustled helplessly, by poetic justice, through an old, old story, to a trite conclusion. The Baron's words, as he closes the library doors, 'We don't want to be disturbed by anyone whomsoever' (p.36), unintentionally summarize the basic precept of these lives. He, his wife, and their circle have striven for appetite-indulgence without emotional or intellectual disturbance. Easy physicality, easily bought, has then called for more recherché means of tensing the libido. Scripted debauch is used for this, until, the Baroness breaking the tacit rules by allowing sincerity to enter into things, another script takes over. Theo, with unconscious accuracy, pinpoints the cause of the commotion: 'The Baroness hasn't been playing the game, and that's about it' (p.57). Previously a product of cosmetic artifice, she has now significantly changed: 'She used to keep her hair frosted or blond-streaked. . . . She shouldn't have let go her shape. Why did she suddenly start to go natural? She must have started to be sincere with someone' (p.57). She has, in fact, 'got sentimental with one of the secretaries' (p.115): which upsets the earlier erotic laissez-faire. This belated switch from perversity to passion is in itself, of course, something of a cliché—as Irene points out, 'she did a Lady Chatterley on him . . . she was really quite typical at heart when it came to Victor' (p.152)—and it merely initiates a different sequence of familiar events. The fatal jealousy—betrayal plot gets underway: and, having let their humanity lapse for so long, those involved have nothing to resist it with—as Lister says: 'They were not prepared for it. They have placed themselves, unfortunately, within the realm of predestination' (p.61). Devoid of individuality, they weakly succumb to pattern: 'He shoots the wife and secretary when they talk too fast. Then he shoots himself, according to the script. He sorts out the mix-up the only way he knows' (p.109). What happens has a retributive rightness. Those unwilling to be disturbed are caught in a deadly drama they cannot disturb. Having lived by fiction, these people are destroyed by it. And out of cheapened lives come cheapened deaths: for, soon the disaster is being plundered by sensation-media, notebooks gulping down salacity while the cameras flash-and-grab. The three dead are buried, as the novel nears its end, under an avalanche of devaluation and the spurious.

In the book, attention is several times directed towards examples of trick photography: scenes edited or cunningly angled so as to appear other than they really are. The bemused Reverend is worked into a couple of these misleading tableaux: ' "Good," says Lister, bringing an elegant silver-cupped glass of softly steaming whisky on a tray from the kitchen, and stirring it with a long spoon. "Do another," he says to Mr. Samuel, standing back meantime, witholding the glass from the Reverend who has begun to stretch out his hand to receive it. The camera clicks smoothly upon the gesture of benediction. Then the Reverend gets his hot toddy' (p.80). And the Baron's rampaging brother frequently requires artistic camouflage, as when, for instance, he is:

> consigned, still wishfully carolling, to the strong arms of Hadrian and Pablo.
> 'Make it look like something,' says Mr. Samuel, training his camera. Immediately they open their mouths in laughter to combine with his, and group themselves on either side of him so that their restraining arms are concealed, only Hadrian's arm of fellowship and Pablo's congratulatory hand in the bridegroom's being revealed (p.124).

This kind of rigging is to occur on an even greater scale with the film of the Klopstock débâcle Clovis has already scripted:

> 'The film's in our pocket,' says Mr. McGuire. 'Our only problem is the casting. You have to have everyone younger than they really are. If Hadrian plays Lister, Pablo could play Hadrian.'. . .
> 'Eleanor can play the Baroness. The same shots as I've got, she only needs to follow the original film and dialogue,' says Mr. Samuel (p.97).

And it is presented as perfectly in keeping, one type of faking merely replacing another: for aristocracy, the book constantly implies, is itself an illusion, totally dependent on setting and indicative of no genuine *noblesse*. Lister and Eleanor, for instance, butler and maid, smartly dressed in the Klopstock drawing-room: 'could be anybody, and more conceivably could be the master and mistress of the house just returned at this time of night from a trip to a city—Paris or even Geneva— or just about to leave for an airport, a night flight' (p.43). Prince Eugene, whose name means 'noble', takes pains to explain, 'I'm not an Excellency, I'm a Highness' (p.61): and what he unwittingly conveys the work endorses. Social eleva- tion, it stresses, is that alone, represents no real distinction. And with the culmination of the novel, the satiric onslaught on the ancien régime—'Let them eat cake' (p.47), Lister has already said of the moribund aristos in the library, and they bear the name of the pro-Revolutionary poet, Klopstock—opens out into a scene of farcically extensive massacre and plebeian invasion. The Swiss Klopstocks perish, with a lunatic inheriting the baronial title and estate; a pregnant housemaid becomes the Baroness; another maid attains the rank of Princess; and, over the ocean in Brazil, it seems that a further branch of the family tree has been violently felled: 'The Butler won't fetch Count Klopstock to the phone. Absolutely refuses. He's locked in the study with some friends and he's on no account to be disturbed' (p.155).

At one of the engineered nuptials where the proletariat help themselves to rich pieces of the upper crust, the wedding march is 'a new rendering of *Greensleeves*, played very fast even at the beginning, and plainly working up to something complex and speedy' (p.121). And, as a witty, intricate and sophisticated variant on a traditional theme, this affords a good image of what Mrs Spark is doing here: just as the portraits in the Klopstock mansion—'cleverly copied . . . from some more probable larger originals' (p.43)—also draw attention to her new satiric strategies. Assembling a miniature tragedy and a miniature horror-tale, she then works elaborate permutations on them, cunningly weaving together ways in which these modes seem necessary and ways in which they appear ludicrously out of place: appropriate to the Klopstocks' social state, perhaps, but grotesquely over-grand for their depleted personalities. And, finally, of course—with the protagonists almost totally obscured by their ostensible subordinates, and such suspense as there is perversely deriving from the possibility of the disaster not occurring—it is the incongruous that predominates. Literary genres, classically employed to arouse pity and fear, or create terror, are here disordered to provoke contempt.

Incongruity does not, however, mean the work lacks symmetry. On the contrary, dealing with people who have attempted to pattern their lusts with fiction, Mrs Spark extravagantly increases her own fiction's already heavy quotient of pattern. The novel is very occasionally allowed to throw out some disconnected bit of life's *bizarrerie*—a pregnant maid, for instance, announcing that death 'must have happened quick' (p.73)—but, for the most part, relevance holds dictatorial sway. Almost nothing is allowed to escape its iron grip. Sometimes, indeed, events already apt enough, such as Heloise's wedding to the deranged heir, have their appropriateness surreally compounded by an additional stroke of deliberately outrageous coincidence. She too, it emerges during the ceremony, is called Klopstock: but thoughts of 'Kindred and Affinity' (pp.48, 129), already summoned by the situation of a nephew amorously involved with his younger aunt, are rapidly dispelled when Lister explains that, despite her surname, Heloise is not related to the noble lunatic. Her father is 'a humble Klopstock, a riveter' (p.130): and even this trade has absurd consonance. Entailing the fixing together of things originally separate, it brings to mind what Mrs Spark is doing in her book, and, because of this, falls into line with other references to cohesion, order, integration: 'We ought to co-ordinate on that point' (p.8); 'it didn't correspond' (p.90); 'only an authority on the subject could have pieced it together' (p.96); 'It's all tied up' (p.103); 'Better straighten things out' (p.107); 'They don't connect' (p.108); 'It's got to compass' (p.114).

Recently, it has been part of Mrs Spark's economy to weigh up new verbal coinages, words and phrases fresh in circulation, and investigate these for what they can yield over and above their current face value. Thus, in *The Driver's Seat*, 'psyche-delic' and 'macrobiotic', already blunted counters in contemporary over-usage, prove, in their pristine sharpness, to have implicit relevance to much more than Lise's dress and Bill's theories: for the book itself makes play with psychedelic—'mind-bending'—techniques, and is concerned with the dearth of macrobiotic—'greatly healthy'—qualities in the society that it portrays. With *Not to Disturb*, Mrs Spark takes a more extensive instance of devaluation: beat jargon—'When you relate you don't ask what you mean. There's such a thing as a trend' (p.89). And, realizing its latent potential—she herself, after all, relates stories by relating events, people, and factors previously unconnected—she scatters this vocabulary, strengthened by a few new mintings, through the cool idiom of Pablo, Hadrian, and Heloise. Their conversation in one scene casually lingers round art and artifice: 'Mr. Samuel is an artist, I'll say that, his perspectives coalesce' (p.93); 'You should always do your own thing in a simulation. It all works in' (p.93); 'Lister never disparates, he symmetrises. . . . Lister's got equibalance . . . and, what's more, he pertains' (p.95). Placed at the centre of the narrative, this episode tactfully provides a light and pleasing resumé of the aesthetic governing the book. Nor do its observations apply only to this work. Mrs Spark's sharply cut perspectives have been coalescing ever since *The Comforters*; with impressive consistency, she has pursued her rigorous purposes through a wide variety of simulations, never disparating, always symmetrizing; formally graceful, these books have equibalance to a high degree; stimulant in content, they very much pertain.

6
Future Conditional

Speaking of *Not to Disturb* in an interview, Mrs Spark once explained, 'There's an element of extravaganza, obviously. One of my motives is to provoke the reader; to startle as well as to please.'[1] In her next novel, *The Hothouse by the East River* (1973), she very much and very deviously continues to deploy aggressively surreal tactics of this kind. Once again, and now in a most drastic way, her technique is that of expectation-jarring parody. To compose this book, several types of literature have been torn apart and their components, clichés and conventions of the mode, cunningly reworked into a collage that is tortuously didactic, calculatedly absurd. Many of the fiction's features are immediately recognizable: what makes its effect disorienting and, indeed, almost hallucinatory is that the pattern into which they would normally fall has been violently deranged. Like a psychosis—and, again, this is a work considerably concerned with lunacy—the novel represents the obsessively insulated development, all rational doubts and reservations being rigorously excluded, of a weird premise.

Dealing with revenants and zombies, death-in-life and life-in-death, *The Hothouse by the East River* is a sinister book: one in which everything occurs the wrong way round. Basically a ghost story, it turns the usual inside out in that here it is the dead who are troubled by spectres of reality, reality of a peculiarly bloodless kind. 'How long, cries Paul in his heart, will these people, this city, haunt me?' (p.104)[2]: but Paul and his wife, though very much more vital than the living who surround them, are long since deceased. And reversal of this kind is repeatedly the fiction's strategy. Its central image is a shadow cast unnaturally, creating darkness where there should be light. Around this bizarre, pervasive emblem rapidly accumulate numerous other instances of normality inverted or defied. There are, for instance, tacit borrowings from contemporary theories of schizophrenia in which 'madness' is seen as sanity, 'sanity' as madness. Much of the action takes place inside a stifling apartment whose inmates swelter in 'the stupe-fying hot air of the winter morning' (p.123). Attention is drawn to photographic negatives in which light is dark, dark light. There is, in long and lovingly attentive flash-backs to 1944, much ironic play with the idea of an Intelligence unit devoted to the propagation of absurdity, of a Security department riddled to a semi-paranoid degree with distrust, anxiety, suspicion. Reference is made to youthful appearance reclaimed in middle age by rejuvenation processes, and *Peter Pan*, drama of retarded juvenility, is travesty-enacted by a group of senior citizens.

'One should live first, then die,' it is remarked late in the book, 'not die then live' (p.142). But for the two main figures of this work the latter has occurred. Prematurely despatched by a rocket-bomb at the close of World War II, Paul and Elsa Hazlett, who had intended to settle in New York once peace was established, are now somehow clinging to existence there. Like a pendulum, the unremittingly present tense narrative swings backwards and forwards between wartime England when the couple were alive and contemporary America where they are dead: and increasingly, as the book proceeds, disturb-ing figures from the violent, vital and impoverished past are propelled in among the deathly, affluence-propped securities of the present. Unable to cope with them, the ego-fabricated afterlife begins to crumble—just as the surrounding city is disintegrating[3]—until the novel ends with the complete demolition of the hothouse and the resigned moving-on of Paul and Elsa, now reconciled and ready to be reunited with the dead.

Like a great deal of Mrs Spark's fiction, *The Hothouse by the East River* functions both as satire and as anagogic exercise. It aims to bring together temporary spuriousness and eternal verity, to amalgamate metaphysics and derision in a tense and tightly plaited structure. And here the common factor is the concept of New York as a kind of purgatory: both metaphori-cally and theologically. On the satiric level, this works fairly clearly. Continually switching between wartime healthiness and the dangerous debilities of peace, Mrs Spark, again making use of inversion, sets the New World and the Old up against each other as if polar opposites: shadow and substance, negative and positive. When Elsa briefly returns to Europe, even though this is sleeked and plutocratic Switzerland, Paul reacts with revealing terror:

> 'Help me!' cries his mind, with a fear reaching back to the Balkan realities. He looks round the room, panicking for her familiar shadow. He wants her back from that wild Europe, those black forests and gunmetal mountains. Come back to Manhattan the mental clinic, cries his heart, where we analyse and dope the savageries of existence. Come back, it's very centrally heated here, there are shops on the ground floor, you can get anything here that you can get over there and better, money's no object. Why go back all that way where your soul has to fend for itself and you think for yourself in secret while you conform with the others in the open? Come back here to New York the sedative chamber where you don't think at all and you can act as crazily as you like and talk your head off all day, all night (pp.89–90).

Europe, when he and Elsa lived there—'Back in 1944 when people were normal and there was a world war on' (p.58)— was a place of open, extreme violence, but it was vitalizing and invigorating: 'In the summer of 1944 . . . life was more vivid that it is now. Everything was more distinct. The hours of the day lasted longer. One lived excitedly and dangerously'(p.34). Present-day New York is the antithesis of this. Though there is violence—lurking in doorways, spilling round the gutters of the rich—the aimed-for norm is money-bolstered ease, nature held at bay by finance in a world of artificially controlled environments, rejuvenating operations, stimulant or tranquillizing drugs, a world where personal problems are complacently farmed out to the appropriate hired aiders—in particular, psychiatrists, for this is: 'New York, home of the vivisectors of the mind, and of the mentally vivisected still to be reassembled, of those who live intact, habitually wondering about their states of sanity, and home of those whose minds have been dead, bearing the scars of resurrection' (p.12). It is also, as one of its denizens remarks, 'a fun city' (p.132), remorselessly hectic. Elsa, familiar with St Augustine, thinks of it as Carthage, chilly 'cauldron of unholy loves' (p.13), passionless involvement and unmoved excess. Symptomatic figures of its life-style are 'those high steel structures' (p.9), Paul and Elsa's children, Katerina and Pierre: a hyper-urban couple, cool as their apartments, never ruffled, never shocked, never emotional, their unvarying response to life an even, slightly bored, vaguely contemptuous hedonism. When Elsa arrives at the very off-off-Broadway theatre in her provocatively bourgeois first-night trappings—rubies and diamonds and an evening dress in flame-coloured crepe,

> She is already causing a stir, but Pierre looks at her languidly, as one well accustomed to absorb any shock. Katerina sways a little, stands lankily upright for a moment, then leans back on bulky Peregrine. 'Am I on a trip or is she real?' Katerina says.
> 'Both,' says Elsa (p.106).

Blasé, chic automata, these imperviously hip metropolites stand as total and deliberate contrast to young Paul and Elsa valuably pained by love and jealousy 'in the green depths of England' (p.135) in 1944. And, of course, Pierre's facilely camp version of *Peter Pan*, another work in which a shadow causes trouble, offers both a comment on New York society and a reflection of it: a comment in that it springs from a dulled craving for perverse novelty—'Sick is interesting. Sick is real' (p.109)—and a reflection in that the Manhattan of the novel is just as much a Never-Never Land—'Now is never, never' (p.59), thinks Paul at one point—as that of the play. There is in both the same refusal to grow up.

And if New York contains many examples of extravagantly fostered immaturity, the novel provides an even stronger instance of this in Paul Hazlett's reluctance to accept mortality. 'To die will be an awfully big adventure',[4] it is claimed in *Peter Pan*. Ambitiously, *The Hothouse by the East River* sets out to explore one such adventure, to suggest the kind of dreams that come in the sleep of death. Paul and Elsa have wanted to make a new life for themselves after the war, and in a very extreme sense they have now achieved this. But their hothouse, an imagined, artificially preserved existence, is precarious. 'It was you,' Elsa tells Paul, 'with your terrible and jealous dreams who set the whole edifice soaring' (p.113): and it is his doubts and insecurities combined with her psychic guerrilla tactics that increasingly undermine and finally demolish it. In a way that threatens Paul, Elsa too begins to fabricate, to play games with the conditional. Things get out of control, rather like the central heating in the Hazletts' apartment that resists all moderation. A scene from Elsa's trip to Zurich points to what is happening: ' "There are English tourists here en route to somewhere," Elsa says. "I passed their table last night and heard one of them saying 'Jonathan's O-levels . . .' That was all, but Christ, it made me want to be sick. The English abroad are so awful and they always bring their own life with them. I mean, what's the use of going abroad if you don't get new life from it?" ' (p.88). Elsa and Paul, also en route to somewhere, have gone abroad to get new life: but, more and more, their old life dogs them. Helmut Kiel, magnet of erotic interest for both, reappears and re-awakens old suspicions and anxieties. What Paul thought of as paradise and stubbornly tries to preserve as such becomes a purgatory in which he writhes, self-gnawed by paranoia. And it is here that Elsa's deviant shadow falls, as it were, into place. Dante, in the *Purgatorio*, perturbed the shades when his shadow revealed him to be in a different order of existence to theirs. In New York, Elsa's anti-natural shadow serves a similar function: 'Here he is with the colour photograph in his hand and here, again, he holds the negative up to the light. . . . Elsa's shadow falls brown in the photograph, grey-white in the negative; it crosses his shadow and the children's as if to cancel them with one sharp diagonal line' (pp.42–3). Repeatedly, in fact, Elsa suggests the insubstantiality of the actual:

'Sit by one of the other windows, Elsa, for a change.'
'There's nothing to see from the other windows.'
'Well, there's the street, isn't there? And the people, the traffic' (p.15).

Receiving light at sunset from the East, sitting in amused 'company with the Nothing beyond the window' (p.125), she half-inhabits some counter-dimension, a positive to this world's negative. Once again, the technique of reversal is being employed, for what the novel here postulates is an antithetical order of existence in which the physical becomes immaterial, the spiritual substantial. Accordingly, Elsa's two shadows indicate a state of indeterminacy, a hovering on some dimensional brink. Continually looking East for resurrection, she is restless in her purgatory. As in their previous life, Paul is trying to imprison and control her by his fantasies: and so,

using techniques learned from the Intelligence Compound—
'black propaganda and psychological warfare . . . a tangled
mixture of damaging lies, flattering and plausible truths' (p.61)
—Elsa, through varying scenes of ethical farce, fights him
educatively. Before they can leave this purgatory, a place in
which they learn and suffer from the implications of their
earthly deeds, egotism, attachment to the world, and lack of
faith must be completely broken down. What seems like
schizophrenia is therefore made to mount a comic onslaught
upon paranoia: a state of mind in which the unreal appears real
is mobilized against one that is excessively geared to the protection of the self and its frightened purposes. Fiction sabotages
fiction until Paul's personality-sustaining fabrication is in
rubble: 'The upper stories . . . already gone and the lower part
. . . a shell' (p.167).

'There's only one area of conflict left,' Pierre explains in a
scene from this novel, 'and that's between absurdity and intelligence' (p.74); 'we have come to a moment in history,' Mrs
Spark claims, 'when we are surrounded on all sides and
oppressed by the absurd':[5] and what this means for literature,
she argues, is that 'the rhetoric of our times should persuade us
to contemplate the ridiculous nature of the reality before us,
and teach us to mock it'.[6] In *The Hothouse by the East River*,
obedient to this, the major rhetoric employed is one of extreme
absurdity. Mrs Spark has been expressing interest in the anti-
novel for some years now. While totally opposed to its assumptions—'I don't in the least accept the theory of the anti-novel'[7]
—she had already plundered several of its devices for her own
purposes: the present-tense narrative, a purely external, sharp-
edged photographing of events. With this book, she goes
further, producing what is, in effect, an ultimate in anti-novels
since it bears that relationship to traditional fiction that a
negative does to a positive. The anti-novel is frequently
propaganda for the absurd; it assails that bad faith that tries to
find significance in contingency; the world it aims to reproduce
is one of meaningless phenomena, a world in which the mind
seems most authentically engaged in physical observation, the
almost obsessive piling up of concrete data from which,
however, no deductions can be profitably made—a world rather
like that of Colonel Tylden's filing-cabinet: 'packed . . . with
information which would amaze the people it describes, so

true and yet so lonely and isolated are the motionless little facts' (p.134). Mocking contemporary absurdity, attacking another kind of bad faith, *The Hothouse by the East River* agilely outflanks the *nouveau roman* by going much further in the same direction; the anti-novel's favoured strategy, the upsetting of usual literary procedures, is ironically turned against it in that here it is made to fight for necessity, order, and cohesion. It is a standard device of parody to twist or heighten fictional conventions so that what appeared significant is now shown to be absurd. To parody the anti-novel, Mrs Spark makes the absurd become significant.

Nor is travesty, in this book, limited to a parodic tinkering with the rarefied aesthetics of the *nouveau roman*. Other sources, some highly unlikely, have contributed to the fiction's genesis. The basic concept of *Peter Pan*, for instance, is as carefully distorted in the novel as it is in the production at the Very Much Club. What Henry James patented as the International Theme—New World and Old instructively counterpointed—provides another starting-point for variations. And Mrs Spark's economic eye for what there is of value in cheap fiction has now lighted on tales of the unquiet grave and the living dead: restless corpses, spectral vagrancy, 'Shadows. . . . Hysteria. Worms' (p.55). Throughout this account of young mortality are sardonically strewn dismembered bits and pieces from such literature. Bloodless Paul has difficulty saying 'bloody' (pp.15, 125); artificially preserved, he continually calls for ice—'I need more ice' (p.78); and when he panics, 'His heart thumps for help. "Help me! Help me!" cries his heart, battering the sides of the coffin' (p.17). 'All lousy, here' (p.51), shrieks Delia, the Hazletts' maid: and, moments later, worms emerge, wriggling upon the breast of Princess Xavier. Ghoulish ingredients are press-ganged into satiric service: the point being that undead Paul and Elsa blend damningly well into a dehumanized, contemporary Manhattan pullulating with unnatural zombies. Their situation provides a freakish metaphor for what is happening to the city: a creepy and perverse tranquillity breaking down under pressure from the old and suppressed savageries.

Combining oblique satire of this kind with exploratory apologetics, reliant on only intermittently visible parody, constant inversion of the normal, repeated blurrings together of the literal and metaphorical, *The Hothouse by the East River* somewhat resembles the wartime scrambler Mrs Spark refers to at one point: 'a special green telephone used everywhere during the war for secret communications. It is known as a scrambler, because the connection is heavily jammed with jangling caterwauls to protect the conversation against eavesdropping; this harrowing noise all but prevents the speakers from hearing each other, but once the knack is mastered it is easy to hear the voice at the other end giving . . . information' (p.63). It is never exactly easy to hear Mrs Spark giving information in this book, and the distracting fictional din, though loud, is farcical rather than harrowing: but, certainly, there are techniques which, once acquired, make the assimilation of the novel's bulletins appreciably less difficult. And the chief of these, perhaps, is the detection of a kind of subliminal punning, which clarifies both what is being dealt with in the book and why it is constructed as it is. Phrases such as 'underexposed' (p.92), 'on leave' (p.71), 'out of your element' (p.61), references to double-agents, a defectors' compound, speculation in real estate, a nightclub called 'The Personality Cult' (p.145) indicate what is happening with Paul and Elsa: while other fragments of, at first sight, naturalistic debris—a briefly glanced-at photographic negative, the black propaganda from the Compound[8]—provide an imagery explanatory of the fiction's type.

Towards the end of the novel, umbrage-and-jargon-loaded Annie Armitage complains that 'all this infra-paranormalization is too much' (p.131); earlier, too, as Elsa is being hurried to the Very Much Club, a girl tries to block her path, 'saying in a slow solemn voice, "That is too much" ' (p.105): and the prompt—that, in this book, Mrs Spark is sarcastically and deliberately out-zanying the zany—is heard clearly enough. Nevertheless, while many of the work's bizarre procedures are, as it were, armoured in advance by the contention that they represent a guying of the eccentricities of others, it is still possible to feel uneasy about this novel. It is not so much that it is oblique as that, on occasions, it appears unnecessarily and even wilfully so: a construct that demands a daunting pressure of attention before it begins to open up and, at the same time, flaunts its own difficulty of access. 'Oh, how you bore me. . . .' Elsa groans to Katerina. 'So bloody literal' (p.24): and as Garven, the derided psychology-sleuth, plods dispiritedly after her, wily 'Elsa laughs. "He hasn't got his material yet. He's looking for the cause, and all I'm giving him are effects. It's lovely" ' (p.56). From time to time, in *The Hothouse by the East River*, the author herself seems likewise enamoured of her own twisty virtuosity. The book's essential difficulty is decorated by a prankish obscurantism; bits of meaningless patterning are mischievously pushed in among the really structural inversions and distortions—shoes that 'fit like a glove' (pp.5,79); two-shadowed Elsa being trailed by that 'hopeless shadow' (p.80), Annie Armitage. And, while recognizing that doubt, suspicion, lack of certainty are important factors in this work, there are moments when its sphinx-faced reluctance to specify seems merely perverse:

> Paul cannot decide upon his age, the man's features being packed away in flesh.
> His name is Peregrine. Perhaps it is his first or middle name, perhaps his last (p.23).

The novel's miserly clutch on Lilliputian mysteries of this sort is rather alienating.

And, conversely, there are even more disturbing moments when the cryptic whisper is replaced by an over-loud and almost hectoring insistence: for the book is far from uniformly reticent. Despite its secluded rationale and frequently recondite stratagems, *The Hothouse by the East River* is capable of startling by its lack of subtlety, especially when it is a matter of displaying deplored character and custom in contemporary New York. Then, muted intricacy periodically yields to something much more rudimentary. Inhabiting the fiction's teetering complexities and labyrinthine patternings are some disconcertingly crude satiric figures—silly Garven: 'Through Annie I am getting to know you, Paul. It's the secondary associative process of the oblique approach. And through you I have a tertiary oblique approach to Elsa' (p.154): and his eventual mate, crazy Annie:

> My new method is strictly bio-psychological. I locate in the various organs of the body the psychological disorder and I treat the patient strictly on the basis of the defective organ. Right now I'm treating a patient who suffers from schizophrenia of the pancreas. I have a gentleman with a hyper-

introspective bladder complicated by euphoria of the liver. I have under my care a manic-depressive kidney, a cardiac super-ego, a case of hallucinations of the diaphragm and a libidinal spleen. Fixations of the reproductive organs are common. A person can suffer from egomania of the toenails. You name it, I can therapeutise it' (p.155–6).

Lugging the ball-and-chain of the author's contempt, these characters are outstripped by frisky Elsa with an uninteresting ease. For so devious a book, the animus is surprisingly open, the two seeming to have been introduced solely as targets for determined snubbing—rather like the young man at the theatre:

A girl holding a bundle of programmes comes forward to greet them. 'Good evening,' she says. 'I'm Alice.' A young man standing beside her says, 'I'm Ken.'
'Really?' says Elsa. 'You don't look it' (p.106).

Here, as quite often, Elsa acts as jeer-leader: and this overt asperity, authorially endorsed is symptomatic of a new impatience, an exasperated readiness to treat the blatant blatantly. Mrs Spark has, of course, endowed a central figure with aggressive wit before. Caroline Rose, January Marlow, Ronald Bridges, Sandy Stranger, Annabel Christopher occasionally voice some of the author's mockery for her: but in all cases, they do so at the expense of an armed and recognizably menacing specimen of nastiness or nuisance and, in almost all, the malicious energies that they display are themselves called in question. In *The Hothouse by the East River*, on the other hand, things are more simplistic. Elsa is given a safe-conduct pass, shielded by the author, while her victims, sometimes not much more than lumbering caricatures, extravagantly warted, blunder towards catastrophe. Her triumphs are both facile and redundant since those she assails are already noisily engaged in self-destruction, condemning themselves only too clearly out of their own nonsense-fangling mouths:

'The hell with her shadow,' says Annie. 'Haven't we got enough serious problems in this city? We already have the youth problem, the racist problem, the distribution problem, the political problem, the economic problem, the crime problem, the matrimonial problem, the ecological problem, the divorce problem, the domiciliary problem, the consumer problem, the birth-rate problem, the middle-age problem, the health problem, the sex problem, the incarceration problem, the educational problem, the fiscal problem, the unemployment problem, the physiopsychodynamics problem, the homosexual problem, the traffic problem, the hetero-sexual problem, the obesity problem, the garbage problem, the gyno-emancipation problem, the rent-controls problem, the identity problem, the bi-sexual problem, the uxoricidal problem, the superannuation problem, the alcoholics problem, the capital gains problem, the anthro-egalitarian problem, the tri-sexual problem, the drug problem, the civic culture and entertainments problem which is something else again, the—' (p.130).

The cool elegancies of distaste, the razor-blade finesse, and damning, finely attuned mimicry so notable in the preceding books here coarsen into strident overkill. Dealing with rampant imbecility, extreme crassness, gross stupidity, Mrs Spark disappointingly allows her style to slip towards a corresponding flagrancy. While satire sometimes remains at the undeveloped level of caricature, wit can fail to get beyond facetiousness. Some of the fiction's pieces of irony, for instance, fall with an unexpectedly loud clatter: ' "We really lived our life," says Paul' (p.34); or; 'Walk on, Elsa,' says Paul. 'Our life's our own to do what we like with' (p.163). An arch quaintness sporadic-ally draws amused attention to itself:

The telephone rings.
'That's Pierre,' says his mother. 'I know his ring' (p.58).

And there is, throughout the Manhattan vignettes, a general reliance on the superficially bizarre or raucously rumbustious. The cast-list is tricked out with characters whose basic nullity is swathed in eccentricity: an overweight princess whose breasts provide a silk-worm incubator; nude policemen; Delia, the berserk maid; and old, old Melly with her quirky maunder-ings. The graceful plot-manoeuvrings of the previous fiction are permitted to degenerate into free-for-all cavortings, rowdy knockabout like the riot at the Very Much Club or the rough-and-tumble aftermath to Delia's sudden breakdown: 'Paul has got one of Elsa's shoes off and is trying to unstrap the other while Elsa, lying back among the broken china, tugs his black and grey hair. Delia, supine on the sofa, growls through her lower teeth' (p.49).

Not the least of the reasons why *The Hothouse by the East River* has a bewildering effect is the fact that it so strangely manages to be both mandarin and garish, highly sophisticated and relatively crude; a work in which clumsinesses break alarmingly through a web of technical virtuosity; where single words can be invested with a fine, strategic resonance or handled with extreme precision while whole scenes are left comparatively slipshod. Semantic nuance, linguistic possibility, the conditional mood, fictional theory, time, and metaphysics apparently hold the author's interest more than the main sector of reality marked off for scrutiny: and this can mean that while the fiction is engaged in self-fondling meditation on the nature of fiction —'If it were only true that all's well that ends well, if only it were true' (p.5), sighs the opening sentence—coarsenesses of content pass uncensored to the forefront. Attention, in this novel, seems unevenly distributed: so that the work's conceptual intricacy is not always strengthened by a similar complexity in its dealings with life.

Not, of course, that *The Hothouse by the East River* is invariably weak on documentary. When the novel's more frenetic fantasies are allowed to quieten, there are scenes of accomplished, naturalistic reportage. Elsa's isolation as inanity and selfishness draw into conspiracy against her is, for instance, registered with a nice accuracy:

> He goes to the kitchen with the coffee-pot and can be heard speaking to Garven. Their voices can be heard, conversing there. The words are undiscernible but the sounds are of an unusual accord. It is like the conversation of men who have shared a house for years and are used to each other's ways; the tones of voice do not reach very high or low registers; there is here and there a little force behind a phrase, as of indignation or resentment, quickly followed by an equal, altogether acquiescent response. The voices lower, as in confidential exchanges. It is like the distant sea. The voices trail away as in reciprocal exasperation (p.114).

And, neatly orchestrated off-stage in this way, the excluding alliance can also be comically choreographed: 'Garven . . . butters his roll and Paul butters his. They eat, they sip their coffee, in unison. . . . Paul pours a second coffee for himself and Garven. "More coffee, Elsa?" he says' (pp.116–7). As usual, Mrs Spark excels in depicting types of solitude, modes of blackmail and betrayal, the mechanics of suspicion and distrust. And, in *The Hothouse by the East River*, this disenchanted ability is of especial relevance: for this is a novel centrally concerned with displaying doubt's corrosive attributes and the attendant need for faith.

Threads connected with this theme run through various aspects of the book—its style, verbal mood, observed psychology, charted behaviour-patterns, scenes of past and present—and are skilfully entwined into strong concordance. The fiction, like all fictions and as its initial statement underlines, is a hypothesis: and, furthermore, a most extreme example of one, in that what it is concerned with is a speculative future being shattered by internal and proliferating possibilities—a kind of conditional civil war. There is, therefore, steady avoidance of the definite, indicative, or positive. The book begins with the word 'if' and ends with a reference to 'unknowing'; its narrative draws heavily on the subjunctive and conditional mood; doubt-indicators like 'perhaps' and 'possible' and 'probably' pervade the text; it is a work in which questions are continually being asked and left tactically unanswered: 'has she decided on this course, or can't she help it? How false, how true?' (p.7), 'Where did she get the money? Where? And what is she doing in this place at this time? . . . In that past there was no word of the future. How has it come about?' (p.142). The wartime sections of the novel, the realistic hinterland to its fantastic future, are clouded by black propaganda; edgy, inter-group mistrust; and a total absence of any real security. In a unit given over to the manufacture of fiction—ingeniously misleading lies, clever hypotheses—Paul, under suspicion himself, speculates about what Elsa may or may not have done. An unsettling state of endless supposition—possibility and dizzying counter-possibility—is established carefully:

> he can only say, 'It's understandable that she hasn't mentioned it.'
> 'And equally,' says Paul, 'understandable that she hasn't mentioned it, if it means nothing to her, going into Kiel's bunker for a lie-down.' He is immediately aware of his error

in uttering that 'if'. He adds, 'Since it means nothing to her' (p.29);

or: 'There is no reason why the man should not look at his watch, but Paul forbears to look back and see whether the man is returning to the gatehouse, there perhaps to telephone, under orders, to report Paul's arrival, and the time of it. It is just possible, it is infinitely possible, even probable, that Colonel Tylden, the security officer, has wanted to find out how far Paul has been put off his stroke' (p.32). The whole atmosphere is sourly steeped in suspicion and reminders of betrayal. The staff of the Compound, as they anxiously realize, are kept under constant surveillance. The prisoners of war have 'ratted on their own country' (p.27); some of these defectors may be double-agents; and one 'speaks with a sort of bitter, convinced pride like a Judas foretelling hell-fires awaiting him as a boastful proof of his betrayed master's divinity' (pp.64–5). The only moments of relaxed rapport are those between Elsa and the collaborators she takes out walking. Then, speaking of their personal histories, sharing their pasts, lessening the mystery about each other as they exchange anecdotes illuminative of their different backgrounds, they briefly achieve a sense of community. This camaraderie is qualified—it partially springs, we are informed, from the 'common misunderstanding that one who does not know another's mother tongue is assumed to be less intelligent and discerning than he is' (pp.63–4)—but it still provides a revealing contrast to the nervous strain under which the Allies in the Compound live.

When the scene moves to New York and the conjectural future, what things could have been like for Paul and Elsa, all this is surreally heightened and distorted. Subdued to what it's worked in, like the dyer's hand, Paul's nature has to be purged of its lingering suspicions and egocentric anxieties, brought around to trust. The novel's major doubter, he is appositely placed in no abiding city—'New York is changing' (pp.51, 59)—and with no continuing stay for his tottering self-confidence. His future is even more suspicion-darkened than his past; the jealousy-mirage grows larger; almost every one of his encounters, as he misguidedly and hopelessly tries to find clear proof about his wife, is thickly misted by surmise, ambiguity, and the equivocal. Credulous and lacking faith, racked by fears of an old infidelity, Paul panics from one attempted ally to another. But, craving for balm, his egotistic need to feel omniscient and infallible is increasingly and comically exacerbated. Elsa knowledgeably works upon his paranoia, therapeutically lies to him; with expert placidity, his son provokes disturbance—' "Wonder what?" says Pierre with a sudden stare that betokens, surely, an innocent question' (p.20); casually, Katerina shrugs away emotional-aid importunacy— 'Oh God, what was 1944? It never happened to me' (p.85); even Garven, brought in to provide ego-sustenance by labelling Elsa as abnormal, perfidiously causes fresh alarm by letting his derangement-seeking gaze rest meditatively on Paul. It is only when he abandons his own concerns and is reconciled to Elsa— ' "Come away," Paul says to his wife. "Come away, love". . . . Elsa's hand is in Paul's and he is drawing her towards the door . . . . Paul takes her arm and they go out' (p.144)—that tranquillity is finally established.

Like *The Public Image*, this is a novel that concludes by suddenly presenting one of its symbols from a different angle, thus endowing it with a new and retrospective significance: 'She turns the car, he following her, watching as she moves, how she trails her faithful and lithe cloud of unknowing across the pavement' (p.168). Put to other purposes throughout the book, Elsa's shadow is here made to represent all that Paul does not understand, can never know, about her. Variously, the novel has displayed the impossibility of attaining full knowledge of another person, and the subsequent difficulty that can be involved in coming to terms with the stubbornly residual 'cloud of unknowing', the opaque area of private history and personality-enigma that, like Elsa, every individual trails around with him. The self, it demonstrates, can never hope to find security through complete and final understanding of another person. There will always be the dark shadow—the unascertained and the ambiguous. The only way to achieve peace of mind, therefore, is to become resigned to this and unselfishly make a leap of faith:

What does it matter, Paul thinks, as he feels Elsa's apprehension from where she sits at the opposite angle of Colonel Tylden's desk, half facing both men. What does it matter what there was between her and Kiel, and what Kiel might have been to me? All that matters is that we've been brought together, at short notice, without chance of rehearsal. It's something, Paul thinks, to know suddenly how much trust there is between us. After all, this experience is something (pp.135–6).

Lack of mystery-acceptance, a restive refusal to admit the limitations of our solipsistic jail: these are shown, in *The Hothouse by the East River*, as breeding misery. And Paul's prolonged unwillingness to trust his wife parallels a similar situation with regard to religious faith. An acceptance of the finally irreducible mystery of another personality through love stands, in this book, as the equivalence of an assent to the mysteries of religion through faith. There, too, Mrs Spark would argue, a cloud of unknowing—God's obscured purposes and procedures—has to be accepted; there, too, the ego must humbly recognize the finite nature of its perception-abilities; there, too, peace comes through trust, patience, and a chastened willingness to receive 'the beautiful and dangerous gift of faith which, by definition of the Scriptures, is the sum of things hoped for and the evidence of things unseen'.[9]

The quotation is from *The Mandelbaum Gate*, and there are, in fact, further resemblances between that novel and *The Hothouse by the East River*: a common insistence that 'Knots were not necessarily created to be untied. Questions were things that sufficed in their still beauty answering themselves';[10] a shared, refurbished image, as when amnesiac Freddy tries to grope his way back towards knowledge through 'a cloud of unknowing, heavy with the molecules of accumulated impressions';[11] and a mutual concern with the ways in which human love and religious faith can interact importantly. Similarities of this kind, pulling the two works together in preoccupation despite their very considerable difference in technique, indicate another salient consideration about *The Hothouse by the East River*: that fact that Mrs Spark took a long time to complete it. In a way, this is a fiction that appears out of sequence since it seems to have been at least begun after the completion of *The Mandelbaum Gate*. In an interview which coincided with the publication of that book in October 1965, it was remarked of Mrs Spark that 'Her latest novel is about the Holy Land; her next is about New York, where she now lives for about 10 months of the year in an apartment building near the United Nations':[12] and, speaking in part about this work in progress, the author added, 'I start with a title (the one about New York is called "Hothouse East River") and I go on from there'.[13] With this particular novel, the going on has taken what is, for Mrs Spark, an exceptionally long time: and this perhaps explains why *The Hothouse by the East River*, though not the most successful of her books, is extremely comprehensive, a compressed and involuted anthology of all her most characteristic techniques and concerns. Some weaknesses are on display more clearly here than in any other of her fiction apart from a few short stories: the novel's slightly smug self-preening on its own obliquity; some open impatience; occasional mimetic crudity which means that fantasy, not always very powerfully curbed by the counter-pressure of strong life-observation, can sprawl into an undisciplined and rather precious fancifying. More pervasive in this novel than before, lapses of this kind can, however, still be found in some of the earlier books whenever the control of tone and material is momentarily allowed to slacken. More pleasingly, *The Hothouse by the East River* is also a compendium of Mrs Spark's most insistent themes and literary procedures. Once again, in icily spotlit scenes, she demonstrates human isolation, the aggressions of the civilized and the barbaric, cowardice's tacit war on truth, the panic of the individual faced with death, the terror of self-surrender. Favourite devices re-occur in a varied form. To her already lengthy catalogue of parody artist-figures, for instance—voice-hearers; mediums; epileptics; imperiously organizing school-teachers; psychotics ruthlessly bent on turning life into a scenario for some inner drama—she now adds the schizophrenic weirdly externalizing her problem. Techniques that have proved their worth before are frugally re-employed: concentration on a clearly restricted social circle, the use of a central disruptive to proclaim unwelcome fact. There is, continuing and intensified, various aspects of this being tightly telescoped together, her austere and fine concern for relevance: the seizing of apt times and places for her plots; an artistic annexing of cities to provide symbolic bases for her work; a way of looking at the world that makes it seem extensive, vivid decor beautifully concordant with the patterns her attention has coaxed out of life's confusion. The literary conventions deployed—here,

157

the absurd and the sinister—are also made unexpectedly and satisfactorily apposite: and, a further refinement, even the pervading verbal mood is brought noticeably into the accord, stamped as part of a matching set.

Perhaps, finally, the most impressive fact about Muriel Spark is the way in which she has managed to attain consistency without monotony, increasing compactness without any loss of scope. Ranging widely in the settings and the subjects of her wit-enamelled parables, constantly experimenting, and, of recent years, very much varying the type of fiction produced, she has still rigorously pursued a steady line of development. The impression her books give is of considerable diversity, but they are alike in that, at the root of each, is a twin concern for truth and economy. It is from these things that all the honed and pondered excellencies of her art derive. An expert parodist, she sets out to mutilate with mockery verbal usages that distort fact particularly grossly or malignly; wittily familar with a multiplicity of variously peopled scenes, she shows common patterns of falsity-acceptance running through them all; cities and time-periods, rendered by her in some vivid detail, are also endowed with salience, scrutinized as to how their inner essence can be most effectively displayed, the apparently evanescent being saved by detected aptness. An artistic dislike of waste, the redundant, the inaccurate, a religious striving after harmony and integration: these dictate both what is in the fiction and the shape it takes. Whilst the content of each novel, a differing excursion into the sardonic comedy of human fallibility, is meant to shake complacency, the form, a pattern of redemptive order, offers hope, embodies what is painfully or comically absent from the world portrayed. Compellingly, the diagnosis and the cure are held in counterpoint. In a short story, Mrs Spark once declared that 'whenever . . . monotony and horror start taking hold of people, the artists rise up and proclaim the virtue of the remarkable things that are missing from the earth'.[14] This is what she herself has unwaveringly and very pleasurably been concerned to do: transfiguring the commonplace through a fiction that remarkably combines the witty thrift of an elegant pun with the packed economy of fine metaphor.

Notes

All references to Muriel Spark's novels are to the editions published by Macmillan, London. The books were published in the USA as follows: *The Comforters* (1957), *Robinson* (1958), *Memento Mori* (1959), *The Ballad of Peckham Rye* (1960), *The Bachelors* (1961), *The Prime of Miss Jean Brodie* (1962), Lippincott; *The Girls of Slender Means* (1963), *The Mandelbaum Gate* (1965), *The Public Image* (1968), *The Driver's Seat* (1970), Knopf; *Not to Disturb* (1972), *The Hothouse by the East River* (1973), Viking.

CHAPTER I

1 'What Images Return', *Memoirs of a Modern Scotland* (ed. K. Miller), Faber and Faber, 1970, p.153.
2 'Speaking of Writing—I', *The Times*, November 21st, 1963, p.18.
3 'My Conversion', *Twentieth Century*, Autumn 1961, p.63.
4 *The Comforters*, Macmillan, 1957, p.141.
5 *Memento Mori*, Macmillan, 1959, p.210.
6 'The House of Fiction', *Partisan Review*, Spring 1963, p.80.
7 'The Brontës as Teachers', *The New Yorker*, January 22nd, 1966, p.33.
8 'The House of Fiction', p.79.
9 *Ibid*, p.80.
10 *The Girls of Slender Means*, Macmillan, 1963, p.89.
11 *The Prime of Miss Jean Brodie*, Macmillan, 1961, p.43.
12 *Ibid*, p.43.
13 'My Conversion', p.62.
14 'Writers in the Tense Present', *The Queen*, Centenary Issue, August 1961, p.146.
15 'My Conversion', p.59.
16 *Ibid*, p.62.
17 Iris Murdoch, 'Against Dryness', *Encounter*, January 1961, p.19.
18 Transcript of a Granada Television interview with Malcolm Muggeridge.
19 'The Religion of an Agnostic', *Church of England Newspaper*, November 27th, 1953, p.1.
20 *Ibid*, p.1.
21 *Ibid*, p.1.
22 'How I Became a Novelist', *John O'London's*, December 1st, 1960, p.683.

23 *The Comforters*, p.131.
24 *The Mandelbaum Gate*, Macmillan, 1965, p.181.
25 *Ibid*, p.240.
26 'Bluebell Amongst the Sables', *Collected Poems I*, Macmillan, 1967, p.63.
27 'How I Became a Novelist', p.683.
28 'The Religion of an Agnostic', p.1.
29 'The Go-Away Bird', *Collected Stories I*, Macmillan, 1967, p.325.
30 'The Portobello Road', *Collected Stories I*, p.11.
31 'The Religion of an Agnostic', p.1.
32 Derek Stanford, *Muriel Spark*, Centaur Press, 1963, p.58.
33 'How I Became a Novelist', p.683.
34 'The Mental Squint of Muriel Spark', *The Sunday Times*, September 30th, 1962, p.14.
35 *The Comforters*, p.31.
36 'Conversations', *Collected Poems I*, p.73.
37 *The Prime of Miss Jean Brodie*, p.135.
38 *Memento Mori*, p.210.
39 *The Bachelors*, Macmillan, 1960, p.240.
40 'The Mental Squint of Muriel Spark', p.14.
41 'The House of Fiction', p.80.
42 'The Portobello Road', *Collected Stories I*, p.30.
43 'How I Became a Novelist', p.683.

CHAPTER 2

1 This and all subsequent page references given in the text are to *The Comforters*.
2 *Pick of Today's Short Stories No.4* (ed. J. Pudney), New York, Putnam, 1953.
3 'The Mystery of Job's Suffering', *Church of England Newspaper*, April 15th, 1955, p.7.
4 *Ibid*, p.7.
5 *Ibid*, p.7.
6 *Ibid*, p.7.
7 *Robinson*, Macmillan, 1958, p.95.
8 'The Curtain Blown By the Breeze', *Collected Stories I*, p.40.
9 'Bang-Bang You're Dead', *Ibid*, p.116.
10 *The Mandelbaum Gate*, p.43.
11 'Bang-Bang You're Dead, *Collected Stories I*, p.97.
12 'The Desegregation of Art', *Proceedings of the American Academy of Arts and Letters*, 1971, p.26.
13 *Robinson*, p.145.
14 *The Mandelbaum Gate*, p.18.
15 'Faith and Works', *Collected Poems I*, p.56.

16 *The Bachelors*, p.121.
17 'My Conversion', p.60.
18 'How I Became a Novelist', p.683.
19 Interview with Malcolm Muggeridge.
20 'My Conversion', p.60.
21 *Ibid*, p.61.
22 *Ibid*, p.59.
23 *Ibid*, p.60.
24 This and all subsequent page references given in the text are to *Robinson*.
25 'Yes: in the sea of life enisl'd,
    With echoing straits between us thrown,
    Dotting the shoreless watery wild,
    We mortal millions live *alone*.
        The islands feel the enclasping flow,
    And then their endless bounds they know. . . .
        A God, a God their severance rul'd;
    And bade betwixt their shores to be
    The unplumb'd, salt, estranging sea.'
        ('To Marguerite on Returning a Volume of
            the Letters of Ortis').
26 'The Religion of an Agnostic', p.1.
27 *Ibid*, p.1.
28 *Ibid*, p.1.
29 *Ibid*, p.1.
30 *The Ballad of Peckham Rye*, Macmillan, 1960, p.202.
31 The idea of working sophisticated variations on the conventions
    of a very specific literary genre is later reincorporated into her
    fiction, however.

CHAPTER 3

1 *The Bachelors*, p.241.
2 'How I Became a Novelist', p.683.
3 This and all subsequent page references given in the text are to
    Memento Mori.
4 *John Masefield*, Peter Nevill, 1953; reissued by Macmillan, 1962,
    p.174.
5 *The Mandelbaum Gate*, p.29.
6 'How I Became a Novelist', p.683.
7 This and all subsequent page references given in the text are to
    The Ballad of Peckham Rye.
8 'The House of Fiction', p.80.
9 *Ibid*, p.79.
10 'What Images Return', p.153.

11 'The Religion of an Agnostic', p.1.
12 This and all subsequent page references given in the text are to
   The Bachelors.
13 'The Mental Squint of Muriel Spark', p.14.
14 'My Conversion', p.63.
15 'The House of Fiction', p.80.
16 *Cf.* 'The clock knocked off at a quarter to three
       And sat there yawning with arms stretched wide.
       And it was set going again by nobody,
       It being Sunday and we being occupied.

       Therefore the day happened and disappeared,
       But whether the time we kept was appropriate
       To rend, to sew, to love, to hate,
       No one could say for certain; all that occurred
       Was Sunday, London, bells, talk, fate.'
       'Day of Rest', *Collected Poems I*, p.40.
17 'The Fathers' Daughters', *Collected Stories I*, p.286.
18 *The Ballad of Peckham Rye*, p.114.
19 *Daily Express*, 25th April, 1963, p.17.

CHAPTER 4

 1 'The House of Fiction', p.79.
 2 'Keeping It Short', *The Listener*, September 24th, 1970, p.412.
 3 'Edinburgh's Muriel Spark Hides in South', *The Scotsman*,
   August 20th, 1962, p.4.
 4 This and all subsequent page references given in the text are to
   The Prime of Miss Jean Brodie.
 5 'Keeping It Short', p.411.
 6 Mrs Blaine's admiration for Garibaldi also provides a period
   parallel to Miss Brodie's political enthusiasms.
 7 *Robinson*, p.1.
 8 'What Images Return', p.151.
 9 This and all subsequent page references given in the text are to
   The Girls of Slender Means.
10 'The Desegregation of Art', p.21.
11 *The Mandelbaum Gate*, p.61.
12 Interview with Malcolm Muggeridge.
13 *Winter's Tales No. 9* (ed. A. Maclean), Macmillan, 1963.
14 This and all subsequent page references given in the text are to
   The Mandelbaum Gate.
15 To emphasize this, perhaps, the book contains a number of
   instances of disguise: Barbara is dressed as an Arab servant, and
   as a nun; Abdul, as a Franciscan friar.

162

16 'The Prime of Muriel Spark', *Observer* Colour Magazine,
   October 17th, 1965, p.10.
17 'Keeping It Short', p.412.
18 *Ibid*, p.412.
19 *The Girls of Slender Means*, p.1.

CHAPTER 5

1 *The Girls of Slender Means*, pp.71–2.
2 'What Images Return', p.153.
3 'The Desegregation of Art', p.24.
4 *Ibid*, p.24.
5 *Ibid*, p.26.
6 *Ibid*, pp.23–4.
7 *Ibid*, p.25.
8 *Ibid*, p.26.
9 *Ibid*, p.25.
10 This and all subsequent page references given in the text are to
   The Public Image, Macmillan, 1968.
11 *The Mandelbaum Gate*, p.36.
12 *The Girls of Slender Means*, p.68.
13 *Observer* Colour Magazine, November 7th, 1971, p.73.
14 This and all subsequent page references given in the text are to
   The Driver's Seat, Macmillan, 1970.
15 See, for instance, pp. 16, 21, 46, 72, 124, 126, 155.
16 Examples can be found on pp. 30, 34, 79, 80, 93, 105, 106, 109,
   117, 123, 140.
17 'Keeping It Short', p.412.
18 *The Mandelbaum Gate*, p.188.
19 *Observer* Colour Magazine, November 7th, 1971, p.73.
20 Interview with Malcolm Muggeridge.
21 This and all subsequent page references given in the text are to
   Not to Disturb, Macmillan, 1971.
22 'The Religion of an Agnostic', p.1.

CHAPTER 6

1 *Observer* Colour Magazine, November 7th, 1971, p.74.
2 This and all subsequent page references given in the text are to
   The Hothouse by the East River, Macmillan, 1973.
3 'New York was beginning to decay', Mrs Spark said, explaining
   her move from there to Rome; 'it was getting dangerous, dirty.'
   Daily Telegraph, September 25th, 1970, p.15.
4 J. M. Barrie, *Collected Plays*, Hodder and Stoughton, 1942, *Peter
   Pan*, Act III, p.545.

5 'The Desegregation of Art', p.26.
6 *Ibid*, p.26.
7 *Observer* Colour Magazine, November 7th, 1971, p.73.
8 This propaganda is literally sinister, one of the meanings of that word being 'Of information, advice, etc.: Given with intent to deceive or mislead'. O.E.D.
9 *The Mandelbaum Gate*, p.18.
10 *Ibid*, pp.301–2.
11 *Ibid*, pp.147–8.
12 'The Prime of Muriel Spark', *Observer* Colour Magazine, October 17th, 1965, p.10.
13 *Ibid*, p.10.
14 *Collected Stories I*, p.146.

Index

166